Burnin' Down the House

VALERIE SWEENEY PRINCE

Burnin' Down the House

Home in African American Literature

COLUMBIA UNIVERSITY PRESS / NEW YORK

Columbia University Press wishes to express its appreciation for a donation toward the cost of publishing this book, given to Hampton University in memory of Frank Carmines.

Grateful acknowledgment is given to Steve A. Prince for use of the following:

"When I Think of Home" (linoleum print, 9" x 12", 1998) from the
  Home Series [frontispiece]
"Urban Dirge" (linoleum print, 9.5" x 14", 2003) from the Home Series
"Ghetto Squares" (linoleum print, 8" x 15", 2003) from the Home Series
"Migratory Tracks" (linoleum print, 8" x 10", 2003) from the Home Series
"Pot to Piss In" (linoleum print, 5.5" x 10", 2003) from the Home Series
"I'll Lay My Head on Some Lonesome Track" (linoleum print, 7.5" x 14",
  2003) from the Home Series
"Sugarman Blues" (linoleum print, 7" x 10" 2003) from the Home Series

Columbia University Press
Publishers Since 1893
New York   Chichester, West Sussex
Copyright © 2005 Columbia University Press
All rights reserved

Library of Congress Cataloging-in-Publication Data
Prince, Valerie Sweeney.
Burnin' down the house : home in African American literature / Valerie
  Sweeney Prince.
    p.   cm.
ISBN 0–231–13440–1 (alk. paper) — ISBN 0–31–13441–1–X (pbk. : alk. paper)
PS374.N4P75   2004
813.009'3552—dc22   2004049444

⊗

Columbia University Press books are printed
  on permanent and durable acid-free paper.

Printed in the United States of America
Designed by Lisa Hamm
c 10 9 8 7 6 5 4 3 2 1
p 10 9 8 7 6 5 4 3 2 1

To Amee, who said, "Go!"

Contents

Acknowledgments

How does any work get done except by the labor of many hands? This particular project has been in the making for more years than I generally acknowledge, but it initially crystallized in a single word during graduate school. The word was, of course, "home." I returned "home by the sea" to finish this book and was received into the welcoming arms of so many people—Margaret Simmons, Barbara Whitehead, Lois Benjamin, William R. Harvey, Joann Haysbert, John Alewynse, Joyce Jarrett, Mamie Locke, April Burris, Bradford Grant, Regina Blair, Jacqueline Regina Blackwell, and Amee F. Carmines—who stood tirelessly urging me forward. Amee, in particular, has been my friend and ally, reading and critiquing when no one else was around. My cousin Lois read an early draft and helped me find my own voice. I write of home because I have a family, not untroubled, not without conflict, not romanticized; I come from somewhere.

Over the years of work on this project, many students have inspired me and helped me to better articulate exactly what I mean.

They have endured my obsession with the themes of "space" and "place" and "home." But those at home have endured the worst of it. My parents, Robert and Lurlene Sweeney, are battle-worn soldiers who stood at the ready for me, always doing whatever was required. My children, Imani and Elijah, have learned patience, independence, and strength, having been born to a mother who simply must write. And my beloved husband, Steve, who can make art out of anything, makes it possible for me to do this work day to day. I thank him for the designs that grace the cover and head each chapter. He continues to be my inspiration.

My sister, Maria, her husband, Neil Osborne, and their daughter, Drexel, opened their home to me and endured my endless chatter without complaint on my trips to Cambridge during the last phase of this project. Their generosity and hospitality were invaluable to its timely completion. The editors at Columbia University Press, Jennifer Crewe and Leslie Kriesel, provided invaluable assistance in refining the finished product.

Carlo Rotella also motivated me. As I watched him speak at the MLA convention in San Francisco in 1998, he was a stranger, but during a time when I needed encouragement, his professionalism and intelligence made me hold to my convictions. His words about working until he finds just the right way to express what he means were not lost on me. One can be a hero without even trying sometimes.

Without the inspiration given by the Holy Spirit to lay everything down and to pick up only those things that Christ allows, I would never have been able to bear all the costs of seeing this project through. Most of all, I thank God for being my home in this world.

I would not change a moment of this walk. Although the work is secular, the journey has been sacred.

Burnin' Down
the House

Introduction: A House Is Not a Home

The search for justice, opportunity, and liberty that characterized the twentieth century for African Americans can be described as a quest for home. During the early part of the century, America witnessed the largest mass migration in history. African Americans left the South looking for opportunity promised by the industrial North. The North did offer relief from the despotism of Jim Crow, which was ruthlessly enforced by mob violence, but poverty and

When I think of home, I think of a place
Where there's love overflowing.
I wish I was home, I wish I was back there
With the things I been knowing. . . .

—Charlie Smalls, "Home"

BONO: . . . Searching out the New Land. That's
what the old folks used to call it. See a fellow
moving around from place to place . . . woman
to woman . . . called it searching out the New
Land. . . . Ain't you never heard of nobody
having the walking blues?

—August Wilson, *Fences*

Not a house in the country ain't packed to its
rafters with some dead Negro's grief.

—Toni Morrison, *Beloved*

racism also awaited the migrants in northern cities. Overcrowded
ghettos began to fester with the stench of unfulfilled promises and
the rotting corpses of failed dreams lying unburied and unmourned
upon hard ground. By the mid-twentieth century, Claude Brown
had joined a chorus of talented black writers including Arna Bontemps, Countee Cullen, Claude McKay, Sterling Brown, Lorraine
Hansberry, Richard Wright, Ralph Ellison, Ann Petry, and James
Baldwin, who were already voicing their frustrations. The dream
that Harlem Renaissance author Langston Hughes wrote about
had indeed been deferred. Anger arose as a wall built in defense of

this sacred place of home. Black writers had invested too much to let the ideal die so unceremoniously. Passion for home ran like lifeblood through the African American psyche.

A look back upon the century of African American literature shows that home is ubiquitous and nowhere at the same time. Perhaps that is why authors express the longing for home utilizing the language and the sentiment of the blues. The blues form arose near the turn of the twentieth century out of the privation experienced by African Americans. It gives voice to the frustrations suffered by the masses of black people living in a culture of white supremacy and presents a unique worldview. The blues introduces a logic drawn from African American sensibility that makes the notion of home seem possible in a chaotic world.

Like home, blues expressiveness grows out of paradoxical associations. Its themes are born from the duality inherent in African American culture. In his renowned *The Souls of Black Folk* (1903), W. E. B. Du Bois coined the term "double consciousness" to describe the psyche as it had developed for African Americans by the opening of the twentieth century, a description that can be aptly applied to the formation of the blues as well. As a distinctly African American genre, it reflects the double-mindedness of the culture out of which it grows. In his theorization of the blues, however, Houston A. Baker Jr. is clear in emphasizing its complexity:

> As driving force, the blues matrix . . . avoids simple dualities. It perpetually achieves its effects as a fluid and multivalent network. It is only when "understanding"—the analytical work of a translator who translates the infinite changes of the blues—converges with such blues "force," however, that adequate explanatory perception (and half-creation) occurs. The matrix effectively functions toward cultural understanding, that is, only when an investigator brings an inventive attention to bear. (9)

African American authors like those studied in these pages, and others such as novelists Albert Murray, Ntozake Shange, Alice Walker, Bebe Moore Campbell, and Walter Mosley, have attempted to be such "investigator[s] bring[ing] an inventive attention to bear" through the end of the twentieth century.

Blues expressiveness appears, in the works studied here, as a form that helps individuals as well as the African American collectivity to negotiate contradictory positions. When the material site fails to nurture and to protect, blues expressiveness is given to function as home in its stead. Farah Griffin writes that blues performance "serves as a transitional space, making the transformation from migrant to urban dweller a little less harsh. It does this by providing the stability of 'home,' as well as offering a means to negotiate the 'here'" (54). It becomes a "safe space," in Patricia Hill Collins's language, wherein migrants can seek shelter. Seemingly, the musical and ideological structure of the blues give it the potential to bring order to the chaos of life by finding meaning in otherwise meaningless and dehumanizing circumstances.

Over the course of the next five chapters, I chart the journey toward home through five novels: *Native Son, Invisible Man, The Bluest Eye, Corregidora,* and *Song of Solomon.* By 1940, a lexicon emerged in African American literature that formed the basis of a vocabulary about home. The city, the kitchen, and the womb recur as sites that specifically inform our understanding of an African American sense of home. Each author draws upon these terms. Each novel repeats and revises the sites and each revision inflects them with new meaning. The pattern of home represented in these novels is configured similarly to the blues matrix described in Baker's *Blues, Ideology, and Afro-American Literature: A Vernacular Theory.* While Baker argues that the "black (w)hole," his blues matrix, seems to offer the potential for retreat and regeneration, the "black holes" in the novels are increasingly destructive. Baker's androcentric metaphor of the black hole invokes the notion of home even as it relies heavily upon a metaphor drawn from the female body. However, Baker is content to imagine a matrix with generative power that does not make room for woman.

The black hole, Baker argues, offers a way of reading literature in the context of vernacular culture. He suggests that the language of the folk is the blues, and the blues is conceived within a cultural matrix that subsumes literary experiences and ultimately "gives birth to light":[1]

> A matrix is a *womb* [emphasis added], a network, a fossil-bearing rock, a rocky trace of a gemstone's removal. . . . The matrix is a point of ceaseless input and output, a web of intersecting, crisscrossing impulses always in productive transit. Afro-American blues constitute such a vibrant network. . . . They are the multiplex, enabling *script* in which Afro-American cultural discourse is inscribed. (3–4)

Having defined the blues as a "matrix" that he describes elsewhere as "always already"—an eternal womb existing apart from the female body—Baker evades the responsibility of dealing with the "whole" individual. As a result, he deals with only part of the community he seeks to champion—the whole male and the female "hole." Such oversights have prompted sometimes acrimonious exchanges between Baker and African American feminist scholars. Yet his study can be productively mined for its underlying assumption: a connection between the blues and the womb.

In order to unpack the conflation that reduces the blues, which Baker reads as a sign of material conditions, to the matrix, which is a womb of sorts, we must keep both the material environment and the female body in sight. Baker removes the body in an effort to divert attention from the individual to the general black populace. He looks to the sign of a railway junction, the X, as a mark that indicates the generic "you" (or "me") and serves as a free-floating signifier of black subjectivity. He writes, "Its mark is an invitation to energizing intersubjectivity. Its implied (in)junction reads: Here is my body meant for (a phylogenetically conceived) you" (5). Baker elides the productive space of the womb (within a woman's body) in order to privilege the "vibrant network" that becomes an asexual, creative junction engineered by male hands and encoded as the blues. The railway crossing X stands as a sign of the mother's erasure, which, in Baker's logic, allows a black nation to be brought forth from the void left in place of her *whole* body.

In contrast to Baker's work, which substitutes symbols for the black female body, Hortense Spillers, in her often anthologized

"Mama's Baby, Papa's Maybe: An American Grammar Book," seeks to resurrect the black woman's flesh. On a symbolic level, she suggests that African American identity is developed around the black (she uses the word "captive") womb. Spillers discusses in "Mama's Baby" how slavery shifted the ground upon which black identity was founded away from the notion of the Father, as found in Lacanian theory. Instead, African American identity is built upon the construct of the Mother: because the newborn black child followed the "condition of the mother," the mother reads as the primary symbolic field. Unfortunately, such an identification serves to perpetuate the institution of slavery rather than to give African American women any real power. Yet they have been used as the scapegoat for the black community's numerous ailments since the time of slavery because they are the sole bearers of the black womb. African American female authors Toni Morrison and Gayl Jones explicitly take issue with the logic that reduces the African American woman to her womb and demand—even to the point of dismemberment and murder—that black female subjectivity be understood as distinct from the black womb.

While Baker looks at the slave narratives of the male authors Olaudah Equiano and Frederick Douglass in order to locate the economics of the blues, he cites Harriet Jacobs's *Incidents in the Life of a Slave Girl* to enable a shift from particular individuals (here Equiano and Douglass) to a generic human community. Baker writes, "A community of women, as represented by Linda Brent, controls its own sexuality, successfully negotiates (in explicitly commercial terms) its liberation from a crude patriarchy, and achieves expressive fullness through the literate voice of the black, female author" (55). Not coincidentally, this community consists of women. Baker thus effectively reinscribes the patriarchal domination that Spillers describes as "patriarchal-matriarchy."

Baker shows neither much regard for psychic consequences nor a great sensitivity to the considerably reduced territory in which Brent is allowed to negotiate her liberation, compared to her male counterparts. She is forced to choose her womb—seducing Mr. Sands in order to resist Dr. Flint's advances—and as a result, she gives birth to two children. The consequence of producing offspring is that Brent is further bound to the institution of slavery because she feels responsible for liberating them as well as herself. In order to do so, she is forced to choose a womb again. Rather than setting forth on the adventure that Baker notes characterizes the male narratives, Brent must be "buried" in what Baker calls a "tomb"—which might be read as "womb"—space inside her grandmother's home (53). Her material environment mirrors and reifies her bodily condition.

While Baker suggests in his introduction that he would like to look at the *gestalt,* loosely translated as "whole to the part," he actually makes one part so large that it takes on mythic proportions. Then he goes on to read the part as the whole. The womb becomes the black hole, which, for Baker, functions as a home wherein a man can safely hibernate until such time as he is ready to (inevitably) emerge. Baker's project validates the blues as a viable means of framing literary analysis. Unfortunately, he imagines the blues matrix as an all-consuming black hole at the expense of women. Baker posits the blues as a "womb" able to "give birth" without the complicating presence of the female body.[2]

In the twenty years since the publication of *Blues Ideology,* many scholars have attacked Baker's work as sexist while others have been content to apply his ideas blindly to their own reading of other texts. My effort in this study is not to dismiss Baker's work as antifeminist; however, I am not willing to apply his framework without offering critique. Instead, I attempt to reclaim the matrix as a black female place and suggest ways to explore representations of home in order to expand upon the lexicon used to read African American literature.

This study charts a dual trend. First, it explores the intratextual movement away from material structures toward metaphorical blues expressions, creative responses complementing the built environment that help characters survive. But it is equally concerned with a larger pattern of movement as authors represent the African American quest for home. This intertextual quest reveals a hitherto covert yearning for a primordial home. "Home" begins as a broad term—a universal ideal to which we aspire. Its locus, repeated in *Native Son*, *Invisible Man*, *The Bluest Eye*, and *Corregidora*, has been getting increasingly smaller—from city to kitchen to womb. Home is configured as a vortex, like Houston Baker's black hole, drawing all things into itself. Finally, the whirlwind can bear no more: this vortex is disrupted by an explosive demolition in *Corregidora*. With the house demolished, readers are left to gather the scattered pieces and rebuild, using the blues sensibilities acquired in the journey through the storm.

Unfortunately, it is not easy to recover what has been lost. In *Native Son*, we meet Bigger Thomas in Chicago after his family has migrated from Mississippi. Clearly, their dreams have been deferred. What Bigger knows as home he confronts in the austere façade of the city that restricts his access and constrains his mobility. It is an understatement to say that the kitchenette apartment where he lives with his family is inadequate. But the kitchenette (a kitchen place) is representative of the Southside (a city place), the black assigned section of Chicago, and the restrictions it places upon his life. *Native Son* chronicles Bigger's rebellion against the station and the designation imposed by the spatial politics that declare, "You can't win." In fact, Bigger cannot win. He can't even sing. Bigger has no use for music. Because it seems he has little regard for blues expressiveness, he must use other means—ultimately, destructive means—to reconfigure a home for himself. He reconfigures the Dalton household by murdering Mary and placing her body in the basement furnace. Thus he transforms his assigned place, the Daltons' basement (a womblike place), into the center of the household as the community searches for the missing girl.

In contrast, the character Mary Rambo in *Invisible Man* tempers her poverty and flavors her home with the sound of her blues. Mary runs a rooming house where the narrator stays for a time. Situated by the blues she sings in the kitchen, she becomes a sign of home for the narrator. Unfortunately, the dynamics that govern Mary's house are presaged in the Southern past at Jim Trueblood's cabin. His sordid history as a sharecropper comes forth as a blues tale centering around poverty, rape, and incest. The Trueblood tale is a blueprint that prefigures Mary's house and begins to clarify the connection suggested in *Native Son* between the built environment (kitchen and city places) and the womb. Ellison emphasizes the black woman's womb by linking it to the Trueblood cabin, through the double pregnant figures of Jim's wife and daughter; then he revises Bigger's basement by sheltering his protagonist in his own dark hole (a womblike place).

In each of the novels, home is correlated with the womb; however, the connection and, more importantly, its implications are not made explicit until Toni Morrison's *The Bluest Eye.* The Northern city that marks the encounter for the male protagonists of Wright's and Ellison's novels is not available to a little black girl like Pecola Breedlove. Her encounters with home are dominated not by city streets but by the geographically smaller sites of kitchens. In representing these sites, Morrison demystifies Mary Rambo's blues kitchen. And because Pecola decides that her problems originate in a failure of sight rather than in a failure of sound, she tries to mitigate them with the blues of her eyes rather than the blues of her mouth. The end of the novel reveals the failure of Trueblood's blues as Pecola brings forth her father's dead seed.

In the fourth chapter, I examine the contrast Gayl Jones represents between Catherine Lawson's kitchen experiences in *Corregidora* and Ursa's experiences as a blues singer. Home takes Ursa even further inside than the kitchen, into the place of the female body. However, it does not prove a suitable home, and what was internalized in the site of the womb becomes painfully externalized. Rather than the black (female) place of the kitchen, as it has been designated by the racialized terms of domestic servitude, Jones offers a graphic blues site that "makes room" for home through a traumatic dismemberment. Ursa is left to find the voices, the others with whom she might sing herself a blues home. In so doing, she reconfigures her relationship with both the past and present. Ultimately, it is unclear whether Ursa finds a viable home place. What is clear, however, is that it is not constructed in an isolated act of individual will. If she is to invent a home, it must be constructed in concert with others.

Finally, *Song of Solomon* presents the city as "ghetto"—but not in the sense of Bigger Thomas's segregated and impoverished Southside, nor in the sense of *Invisible Man's* ever-changing Harlem. Morrison signifies on the leitmotif of the earlier novels and reconfigures the places of the city, the kitchen, and the womb in terms that are more viable. The African American quest for home, irresistibly attracted toward increasingly smaller sites, breaks free from the vortex and explodes in *Corregidora*. Morrison gathers the scattered pieces, inverts the pattern, and leads the way out of the womb. It is dead; the kitchen opens outward; and the city becomes ghetto. Rather than being a black place because it is so interior that there is no light, as is the case with Baker's black hole, home becomes a black place because of the presence of all color. To be at home, then, Morrison suggests in *Song of Solomon*, the African American community must embody the blues paradox of holding its opposite within itself. The novel declares that home is untenable— yet it must be defended, even at the cost of our lives.

Notes

1. Baker characterizes the black hole as "The symbolic content of Afro-American expressive culture [which] can thus be formulated in terms of the *black hole* conceived as a subcultural (underground, marginal, or liminal) region in which a dominant, white culture's representations are squeezed to zero volume, producing a new expressive order" (152). Without lodging any specific critique about the model of the "black hole" itself, feminist scholars like Deborah McDowell, Barbara Christian, and Joyce Ann Joyce are not particularly persuaded by his case. Their arguments against Baker largely surfaced as critiques of the value and effectiveness of poststructuralist criticism in the reading of African American womanist texts. Barbara Christian, "The Race for Theory," *Cultural Critique* 6 (Spring 1987): 51–63; Joyce A. Joyce, "'Who the Cap Fit': Unconsciousness and Unconscionableness in the Criticism of Houston A. Baker, Jr., and Henry Louis Gates, Jr.," *New Literary History* 18 (Winter 1987): 371–83. Michael Awkward and Ann du Cille, however, do offer specific critiques. See Michael Awkward, *Inspiriting Influences: Tradition, Revision, and Afro-American Women's Novels* (New York:

Columbia University Press, 1989); Ann du Cille, "'Who Reads Here?': Back Talking with Houston Baker," *Novel: A Forum on Fiction* 26.1 (1992): 97–106.

2. In *Race Men,* Hazel Carby lodges a similar critique in her reading of W. E. B. Du Bois's *The Souls of Black Folk*: "The map of intellectual mentors he [Du Bois] draws for us is a map of male production and reproduction that traces in its form, but displaces through its content, biological and sexual reproduction. It is reproduction without women, and is a final closure to Du Bois's claim to be 'flesh of the flesh and bone of the bone,' for in the usurpation of the birth of woman from Adam's rib, the figure of the intellectual and race leader is born of and engendered by other males" (25–26). See Hazel Carby, *Race Men* (Cambridge: Harvard University Press, 1988).

Works Cited

Baker, Houston A., Jr. *Blues, Ideology, and Afro-American Literature: A Vernacular Theory.* Chicago: University of Chicago Press, 1984.

Griffin, Farah Jasmine. *"Who Set You Flowin'?": The African-American Migration Narrative.* New York: Oxford University Press, 1995.

I had discovered the crowning error of
the city. . . . The city was not the endless
succession of canyons. . . . The city had limits.

—F. Scott Fitzgerald, "My Lost City"

Ain't you heard
The boogie-woogie rumble
Of a dream deferred?

—Langston Hughes, "Dream Boogie"

1

Living (Just Enough) for the City: *Native Son*

The novels in this study span nearly forty years, beginning in 1940 with Richard Wright's *Native Son* and concluding in 1977 with Toni Morrison's *Song of Solomon*. In this chapter I look at *Native Son* because it speaks of home in broad terms that are characteristic of this period of great transition. At the outset of the century the Northern city was presented as the African American's best chance for locating a viable home. And after the advent of the mechanical cotton harvester, World War II, and other mitigating circumstances, many put their hope of finding a home in the North. At the time Wright published *Native Son*, 77 percent of African Americans lived in the South. Over the next 30 years, 5 million of them would move to Northern cities. This is the backdrop of the novel (and of this book). Although his protagonist, Bigger Thomas, is part of this great wave of sojourners, Wright declares that he has natural rights of inheritance. Bigger is a *native* son. He inherits the city, but it refuses him. Many scholars have considered the ways the city fails to be home for Bigger, but I read this topic from a new perspective. *Native Son* introduces a blueprint for home that will be revised by Ralph Ellison in *Invisible Man*, Toni Morrison in *The Bluest Eye* and *Song of Solomon*, and Gayl Jones in *Corregidora*.

Read chronologically, the novels show the African American longing for home as a pattern of movement, first to the outdoor place of the city, then to the indoor place of the kitchen, and finally, to the quintessentially interiorized place of the womb. Southerly winds blew African Americans away from Southern ground. Even if they had not been persuaded by the façade of the "Promised Land," many migrants believed life in the North could not be worse than the conditions they experienced in the South. In fact, if half of what they heard—from fast-talking Northern industrialists about wages and from recent migrants bragging of new conquests—was true, the North was a free train ride to a land of opportunity. For a time, the Northern city stood as the symbol of home's potential. So migrants went north in search of their dreams.

By 1940, when Wright published *Native Son*,[1] a generation of African Americans had been raised in Northern cities. Wright had migrated as a child, and his work reflects the disillusionment characterstic of novels like *The Street* by Ann Petry, *Home to Harlem* by Claude McKay, and *God Sent Sunday* by Arna Bontemps. African Americans had discovered that the potential embodied by the city was bounded.

In *Native Son*, Bigger's experiences with the city are in the foreground. Nevertheless, the kitchen, configured as both the kitchenette apartment and a place within the Dalton household, plays a vital role. The kitchenette provides a sharp contrast to Bigger's experience in the city streets. The womb in the novel is less obvious. The Dalton basement, Bigger's assigned place, is a womblike place from which Bigger hopes to emerge into a new life. However, the city refuses to accept Bigger's claim of belonging and forces him to occupy increasingly confined places.

Kitchen: The Kitchenette Apartment

The opening "Brrrrrrriiiiiiiiiiiiiiiiiiinng!" awakens the Thomas family. The harshness of the tone sets the mood for what will follow. The kitchenette apartment at the beginning of *Native Son* is restrictive for Bigger as well as the other members of his family living there. This place introduces the tensions at work in the built environment that will frustrate Bigger's aspirations. Our attention is drawn to Bigger and his natural (male) desire to escape the stultifying (female) place of the apartment. Segregationist housing practices forced African Americans in Chicago to live in such ghetto kitchenette apartments. Wright describes the social dynamics this fostered in *12 Million Black Voices*: "the kitchenette throws desperate and unhappy people into an unbearable closeness of association, thereby increasing latent friction, giving birth to never-ending quarrels of recrimination, accusation, and vindictiveness, producing warped personalities" (108). The kitchenette places tangible and intangible boundaries around the lives of its inhabitants. These barriers constrain their growth and restrict their movements.

A narrow space of one room is the Thomases' living area. The living space is so contained by the kitchenette that it leaves the natural connections between mother and son, brothers and sister distorted, if not completely compromised. As Dan McCall states, "Wright's point [in representing the kitchenette] is not to deny the Negro's 'folk culture.' He was trying to show that for those slum dwellers the folk culture was swallowed in unbearable closeness" (7). The architectural design maximized (white) profit and almost completely neglected (black) human needs. Bigger's effort to draw invisible, defensive curtains around himself for protection and privacy cannot help but violate others' personal boundaries. People living in this household are simply pressed too close.

Bigger has difficulty identifying with those around him. His mother nags him in lieu of his deceased father to take a relief job in order to help make ends meet. Bigger sees her as another obstacle to control over his own life. Poverty and anger constrain him and limit his ability to interpret his experiences more productively. The problem that arises out of these circumstances, as Keith Gilyard points out, is that Bigger "cannot give voice to either his rage or his vision" (158–59). His frustrations have few expressive outlets. Once Bigger loses respect for his family and their cultural practices, he loses sight of a vital resource. Although limited, Mrs. Thomas is rooted by her participation in expressive practices. Constricted as he is, Bigger does not recognize folk culture as such and thus can only mock folk practices that might otherwise serve as emancipatory gestures. This mockery is evident in the exchange Bigger has with his mother over breakfast:

> "Bigger's setting here like he ain't glad to get a job," [Mrs. Thomas] said.
> "What you want me to do? Shout?" Bigger asked. (15)

Mrs. Thomas is contemptuous of Bigger because, unlike his sister, Vera, he does not share her limited aspirations and is not satisfied by the offer he has received for a relief job. The sarcasm Bigger expresses here is eclipsed by irony later as the significance of this exchange is highlighted by his unexpected "shout"— manifested as Mary's homicide. For Bigger, his mother—like Bessie, the girlfriend he later murders in cold blood—embodies folk culture.

While to the uninitiated, Bigger may appear to be asking his mother if she wants him to yell (speak in a loud voice), Bigger is really asking if she expects him to perform a shout. A shout is a particularly African American expression of joy, gratitude, and praise to God, wherein one dances with religious abandon. Anthropologist Zora Neale Hurston reads the practice of shouting in *The Sanctified Church*:

There can be little doubt that shouting is a survival of the African "possession" by the gods. In Africa it is sacred to the priesthood or acolytes, in America it has become generalized. The implication is the same, however, it is a sign of special favor from the spirit that it chooses to drive out the individual consciousness temporarily and use the body for its expression. (91)[2]

Practiced widely in Holiness and Pentecostal churches popular among Southern migrants,[3] such charismatic expression is far more active than a mere outburst. Instead, as Hurston notes, "Shouting is a community thing" (91) that engages an individual as part of a congregation in fellowship with God. Bigger has no intention of expressing joy, particularly not in the form of a shout, over the offer of a relief job. He views shouting as frivolous. Thus he cuts himself off from a potentially meaningful engagement with this community within the household.

An effective exploration of home in *Native Son* begins with an understanding of the social dynamics at work in the kitchenette. The material constraints the kitchenette imposes upon Bigger mold his sense of home, and not simply by instigating his alienation from expressive gestures; there is also a clear division between genders. The kitchenette is designated as female by the dominance of Mrs. Thomas's myopic worldview. Mrs. Thomas and the home she represents cannot accommodate the lifestyle that Bigger wants. In the opening scene when a black rat invades the apartment, fear of exposure, embarrassment, or shame are all put aside for the immediate concern. The women huddle together as Mrs. Thomas locates the rat: "Frantically, Vera climbed upon the bed and the woman caught hold of her with their arms entwined about each other, the black mother and the brown daughter gazed open-mouthed at the trunk in the corner" (8). From the bed, she directs her son toward the threat. Bigger's role as "man" thrusts him into the position of defender of his home place; conversely, Vera and Mrs. Thomas's role as "women" suggests that they are defenseless. These roles are rigidly imposed and further demonstrate the impermeability of the space. It is Bigger who must kill the rat, and so he does. Wright utilizes this fierce imagery to foreshadow what is to become of Bigger himself. The dynamics inside the apartment are but a reflection of larger social forces.

The sense of triumph produced by Bigger's defeat of the rat is short lived, as his attempt to be "the man of the house" ends with this primal act of aggression. The "house," from Bigger's perspective, is hardly worth defending. Yet Bigger acts, as opposed to the inaction of his sister. He operates from the perspective that he will make a difference in this situation. On the other hand, Vera is so afraid of the rat that she cannot even think to jump onto the bed. Instead she shrinks into a corner until her mother orders her to move. Clearly, this is not the first encounter this family has had with a rat, nor, the novel also implies, will it be the last; yet Vera has not found an active way to manage the situation. Trudier Harris explains the gender dichotomy as part of a larger schema of oppositions:

> Wright sets up an opposition in the novel between the native and the foreign, between the American Dream and American ideals in the abstract and Afro-Americans trying to find their place among the ideals, between Bigger as a representative of something larger and freer, indeed more American, than the limitations of the black community and the black women as representatives of a culture and a way of life that would stifle such aspirations. (63)

Vera is paralyzed to the point of utter vulnerability and is, therefore, completely subject to the forces of her environment. The rat is an imminent threat to the family and they know it must be killed.

The rat race begins here for Bigger in the kitchenette, the lived reality of black life within the ghetto. Bigger is not really invested in protecting his family. In fact, he considers this place a threat to his own emotional well-being:

> He hated his family because he knew that they were suffering and that he was powerless to help them. He knew that the moment he allowed himself to feel to its fullness how they lived, the shame and misery of their lives, he would be swept out of himself with fear and despair. So he

held toward them an attitude of iron reserve; he lived with them, but behind a wall, a curtain. And toward himself he was even more exacting. He knew that the moment he allowed what his life meant to enter fully into his consciousness, he would either kill himself or someone else. So he denied himself and acted tough. (14)

Vera and Mrs. Thomas are living behind a "curtain" that obscures their ability to see the mechanisms operating in their world to control them. But in this passage, we find that Bigger also lives behind a curtain of sorts—a wall of "iron reserve." In the absence of physical walls set in place to make a space livable—for example, to separate male and female sleeping areas—Bigger's barrier of "iron reserve" is a defensive boundary he erects in an attempt to protect himself from the debilitating realities of his life. These barriers reconfigure the space of the apartment and serve to direct Bigger's movement through it.

But there are moments when Bigger's barrier fails him. His mother's voice transgresses this ephemeral border and reaches Bigger from behind her curtain as she sings:

Life is like a mountain railroad
With an engineer that's brave
We must make the run successful
From the cradle to the grave. . . . (14)

This song evokes the image of the junction—a crossroads of movement through territory that evokes the image of the South. Significantly, the song she sings is a gospel, but the hope of Christ as Savior is absent from the segment represented here.[4] Instead, her song charts the challenges and potential triumphs of life in terms of geographical markers. Success is measured by one's ability to negotiate the spatial obstacles and to move from one site to another. To change locale, then, is to change one's relationship to the world. Rather than appearing as a form of praise or worship centered around the figure of Christ (since Christianity is the implied context) that would mark her text as sacred, Mrs. Thomas's music functions like blues. The train, a common symbol of the blues, suggests both the hope embodied by arrivals and the sorrow found in departures. Her song helps her negotiate the here and now that is circumscribed by the historical context of migration.

The song irks Bigger, and he is glad when she stops singing and returns to him with a pot of coffee and a plate of crinkled bacon (14). Bigger is not consoled by the superficial comfort offered by his mother's song. He focuses instead on the immediacy of his physical hunger. His unfulfilled desires within the stultifying environment of his home are assuaged momentarily by food.

In an effort to escape the constrictions of the kitchenette, Bigger expands his sense of home to incorporate the masculine space of street culture. "Domestic space is stifling and provincial," according to Farah Griffin's reading of male migrant characters. She continues, "The male migrant characters of . . . [particular migration literature] attempt to develop a street culture and/or attempt to acquire a critical consciousness as a means of resisting the negative impact of the city" (123). In many ways, the street culture these characters develop is antithetical to the maintenance of home and family. But as Wright demonstrates, the kitchenette does not adequately sustain that family either. It fails to be home, a shelter from the inhospitable city, so the culture of the streets is established to fill that role. Ironically, Bigger's soulish longings are a more complicated manifestation of the expressions of hope about which Mrs. Thomas sings. In their own ways, both of them have invested place with so much yearning that they believe it might yield the route to their liberty. So Bigger goes outside to try to catch a glimpse of what it means to be at home.

City: The Street

Just after the novel's opening scene, Bigger exits his apartment and goes downstairs before going out into the morning. He stops to smoke a cigarette and watches two white men putting up a billboard across the street and talking of politics. Their discussion reveals the presence of an invisible class structure that separates blue-collar workers like themselves from politicians like Buckley, who is pictured on the billboard: "I bet that sonofabitch rakes off a million bucks in graft a year. Boy, if I was in his shoes for just one day I'd *never* have to worry again" (16). At the same instant that their work reveals the distance between themselves and men with power and money like Buckley, it also suggests Bigger's societal position in relationship to them all.

Bigger's sense of home has been predetermined by a system that predates him and relies upon his subjugation for its existence. In "Richard Wright and the Dynamics of Place in Afro-American Literature," Houston Baker posits a reading of place that coheres with this reading of home for Bigger. As a subset of place, home is subject to the dynamics and politics associated with it. Reading the significance of location, Baker writes:

> For place to be recognized as actually PLACE, as a personally valued locale, one must set and maintain the boundaries. If one is constituted and maintained, however, by and within boundaries set by another, then one is not a setter of place but a prisoner of another's desire. Under such conditions what one calls and perhaps, feels is one's own place would be, from the perspective of human agency, *placeless*. Bereft of determinative control of boundaries, the inhabitant would not be secure in his or her own space but maximally secured by another. Such confinement is always a function of interlocking institutional arrangements. ("Richard Wright" 87)

Baker's assertion is that the notion of place originates within the primary displacement of the slave trade wherein African peoples were dispersed as property throughout the white, western world. Without the fundamental acknowledgment of human agency, African Americans were left to circulate under the control of economic institutions in the same manner as any other resource. Baker argues that place for them "begins in a European DISPLACEMENT of bodies for commercial purposes" ("Richard Wright" 91). While I am less interested in the economics than in issues concerning race and gender, Baker's Marxist reading works well with Wright's communist slant.

The hands of these two white men literally bring Buckley's visage into Bigger's daily life as a sign of the "true" policing power (unlike the critical watch of someone like his mother). Operating on various levels, white society has the authority to post signs of that power throughout culture. The accusatory glare follows passersby who fall beneath the point of the finger as the billboard revises the standard World War II motto of "Uncle Sam wants you" with its own variation: "IF YOU BREAK THE LAW, YOU CAN'T WIN!" (16–17). Although the billboard will randomly accuse *every* viewer with the same glare, the politics associated with location guarantee that some groups of individuals will be addressed more often than others.

Still, the street culture Bigger participates in with his male friends seems to offer a less restrictive alternative to life inside the kitchenette. On the street or in the pool hall that is an extension of the male street culture, Bigger is able to conjure up defiant visions of robbing a white man's store or of becoming an airplane pilot. In these spaces he can think bigger thoughts than those his mother could ever imagine. His dreams are understood and even shared by Gus and the others. This masculine culture is set in contrast to the purportedly female dominated space of the apartment. Men and boys can gather and scheme without the policing eye of frightened women like his mother and Vera.

In the street spaces, Bigger and his friends plan a bold robbery of a white man's store, but like the women, these boys are scared. Bigger foils the planned robbery before it can begin by attacking his friend, Gus—masking his fear under the guise of anger. Although he is able to maintain his masculinist front with his friends and, by extension, male street culture in general, in this act he succumbs to another thinly veiled level of white oppression.

Like the kitchenette apartment, which only offers Mrs. Thomas imaginary power in exchange for effective control, the street is yet another realm of white domination. It seems to expand the constrictive boundaries of the kitchenette and give Bigger the chance to lust after the freedom suggested by flight. While standing in the street, Bigger spies a plane and recognizes that a lack of opportunity rather than a lack of ability keeps him from flying, too. But Gus reminds him of the other barriers that Bigger neglects to consider: "If you wasn't black and if you had some money and if they'd let you go to that aviation school, you *could* fly a plane" (20). The cinema, airplanes, and billboards serve as constant reminders of his allotted station in life. Bigger is not freer on the streets. The black street culture pictured here by Wright is as limited and limiting for men as the kitchenette apartment is for women.

All around Bigger as he stands talking with Gus on the street, people are moving. The seemingly purposeful action of vehicles, birds, and people captivates him: "Automatically, his eyes followed each car as it whirred over the smooth black asphalt. A woman came by and he watched the gentle sway of her body until she disappeared into a doorway" (19). As Bigger and Gus stand on the street "playing white," they are set apart by the seemingly goal-directed movement around them.

Invoking the rich history of the dozens, a mean contest of wit and words, played on porches and in outdoor, street places, this game of "playing white" holds the potential to serve as a blues moment. Such a moment occurs when one is able to translate painful experiences through a filter of African American expressive culture in order to impose meaning upon potentially devastating contradictions. For instance, Mrs. Thomas's singing serves as a blues moment because she is able to glean some meaning and a measure of comfort from it in the midst of a difficult situation. Bigger's efforts to use folk expression are thwarted, however. The men's play finally gives way to frustration, resentment, anger, and fear. Bigger's effort to reencode his position within the world through this game with his friend is ultimately no more consoling for him than his mother's (blues) singing. Finally he tells Gus: "It's just like living in jail. Half the time I feel like I'm on the outside of the world peeping in through a knot hole in the fence" (23). Bigger has no expressive vehicles through which to either effectively articulate his feelings to those outside his small circle of friends or reinterpret and affirm the value of his life and his experience.

He dismisses the value of his common black experiences—as evidenced by the movement of the community passing by him—in favor of things outside his grasp: flight, material wealth, and the power signified by "whiteness." The meaning of the movement in the streets is lost on him. Instead he is a bystander as others move about. He cannot help noticing this movement, but his gestures toward expression in the play with Gus fail to engage him in the surrounding action, reinforcing Bigger's disengagement from the community. Community, an expressed connection between human beings, is vital to the institution of home. Without such ties, an individual like Bigger is unlikely to build such a place on his own.

While the street may feel more like home in that it is less provincial than the apartment, for Bigger, it is also a place that stifles his creative expression and restricts his ability to engage others in meaningful ways. After sabotaging the planned robbery of Blum's store, Bigger must take the relief job his mother wanted for him as chauffeur for the Dalton family. In this way Bigger moves from the kitchenette apartment and the streets to the Daltons' house, a kitchen place that begins to introduce a connection to the womb.

Between the Kitchen and the Womb: The Dalton House

After the kitchenette and the streets of the Southside fail to provide adequate shelter, it is doubtful that the Dalton house will meet Bigger's needs. In some ways, his sense of place expands as he takes the trek across the city to the Dalton household to accept the chauffeur position. The job gives him justification for going into a prohibited part of town. But his place within the Dalton household as servant mitigates any perceived expansion. Instead, Bigger's sense of place becomes smaller. Although he will venture back into the Southside after his murder of the socialite Mary Dalton is uncovered, his encounter with this household seals his fate. The city closes in and his sole expressions of power are forged out of his experiences there.

Despite the liberal sentiment that is the subtext of the relief job offer, apart from his naïve hope that the Daltons might be like the whites in the movies, Bigger finds no reason to share his mother's optimism about his new employment. As James Giles astutely notes, "Mr. and Mrs. Dalton primarily represent a devastating satire of misguided, white liberalism. They attempt to atone through meaningless philanthropic gestures for their guilt as exploitative capitalistic landlords. By doing so, they succeed only in temporarily confusing black rage and, thus, delaying essential social reform" (80). Over the course of the novel, it becomes evident that hiring Bigger is one of those "philanthropic gestures." The shallowness of their actions implicates the Daltons in a system of oppression that victimizes Bigger. John M. Reilly connects the Daltons' social position to their race politics. In their apparent naïveté, they partner with more blatant forms of racist oppression:

[The Daltons'] responsibility for institutionalizing racism through the exploitation of their tenants and the enforcement of segregated housing patterns cannot be attributed directly to their characters, in the way that Britten and Buckley may seem to be motivated by race hatred. Yet, as the logic of the novel shows, the Daltons' complicity in exploitation is a greater evil than the Klan-like behavior of Britten or Buckley, for their controlling role in the economic and social system of Chicago creates the conditions that frustrate and oppress not only the Thomases but all blacks in the city, conditions that in turn require the active reinforcement of the overt racism that the Daltons are too respectable to indulge, too self-deluded to acknowledge as necessary to the maintenance of their social position. (43)

The Daltons' sense of home (and place) grows out of their economic authority, which requires policing by spatial directives such as the billboard outside the Thomases' kitchenette apartment.

As landlord, Mr. Dalton knows neither the people nor the circumstances of his property. He does not even seem to know the addresses of his holdings. Thus the sincerity of his liberal concern demonstrated through his gifts of Ping-Pong tables and offers of menial jobs to black people is undermined by his detachment as landlord. This dynamic is evident in his brief exchange with Bigger.

Shortly after meeting him, Mr. Dalton inquires about Bigger's living conditions:

> "How much rent do you pay?"
> "Eight dollars a week."
> "For how many rooms?"
> "We just got one, suh." (50)

Mr. Dalton's line of inquiry places Bigger's family under a microscope that mirrors his daughter's later, more obviously offensive assertions. Mary Dalton more directly expresses:

> "You know, Bigger, I've long wanted to go into those houses," she said, pointing to the tall, dark apartment buildings looming to either side of them, "and just *see* how your people live. . . . They're *human*. . . . There are twelve million of them. . . . They live in our country. . . . In the same city with us. . . ." Her voice trailed off wistfully. (70)

Mary speaks of the black belt, the African American's assigned portion of the city, as if she is rendering a dream world created not through interrelating systems of power, access, and control but through her own naïvely dehumanizing imaginings.

While attempting to orient Bigger to his new job, the Daltons' housekeeper, Peggy, tells him, "It's really more than a job you've got here. . . . It's just like home" (58). It *is* just like home, inasmuch as home overtly and covertly restricts access and constricts movement. Bigger's place there is, after all, a room in the back, above the kitchen, entered through the basement. This place can be home for him as long as he remains confined within these parameters. (Of course, it is the transgression of those boundaries and Bigger's fear of being discovered in a white lady's room that compel the action of the novel and literally frighten Bigger to the point of murder.) Yet, for a brief moment, there is potential for Bigger to ally himself with this household.

As in the earlier scene that day when his mother brings him breakfast, food helps satiate Bigger's feeling of longing. The temporary satisfaction of eating fosters a sense of connectedness that is necessary in the establishment of home. After Bigger eats the food Peggy prepares for him, he succumbs to the pleasure of the moment: "He had quite forgotten that Peggy was in the kitchen and when his plate was empty he took a soft piece of bread and began to sop it clean, carrying the bread to his mouth in huge chunks. . . . He stopped chewing and laid the bread aside. He had not wanted to let her see him do that; he did that only at home" (56). The problem that Bigger experiences here, as in the earlier scene, is that the comfort only lasts for a short while; the sense of alienation returns to him after the food is gone.

In a similar scene in *Invisible Man* the narrator is reminded of the South while eating hot, buttery yams from a street vendor in Harlem. But the kind of connectedness that the invisible man feels is not sustained here because Bigger does not acknowledge or accept the importance of such affiliations. Unlike the invisible man, who desires to return to his roots in the South, Bigger is clearly detached from his Southern past. He is able to emotionlessly recount the fact of his father's murder to Jan and Mary in the same detached way that he steels himself to his family's conditions in the kitchenette. And only rarely, in moments involving food or song, does Bigger seem to have even a glimmer of recognition of his heritage.

Bigger returns to the Southside with Mary and her boyfriend, Jan. However, his experiences there are permanently altered by the events that occur after his initial encounter with the Daltons. The Southside, the kitchenette, and the Daltons' basement are enclosed by monolithic walls that Bigger's rage alone is unable to surmount. The friction between him and Mary ignites anger in Bigger that must find expression. Otherwise, Bigger cannot start the creative task of building useful shelters. Instead of creativity, his anger finds the wrecking ball of violence. Alienated as he is, Bigger is not able to effect enough of a change to dramatically alter the African American experience of home. The walls erected to contain him remain unmoved even as Bigger's fate is sealed.

City: The Black Belt

Bigger's efforts are generally to disassociate himself rather than look for ties that might bind him to other people. Perhaps this inclination fuels his contempt for Mary, who makes foolhardy attempts to pronounce her solidarity with him upon their initial meeting. Instead of provoking kinship, her unmerited trust elicits his confusion. Consequently, whatever impulse might be motivating her demonstrations of concern for black people is undermined by her lack of insight into Bigger's individual character. Without sincere acknowledgment of his humanity, her behavior toward him is both asinine and offensive. For example, while in the car with Bigger, a drunken Mary begins to sing:

> Swing low, sweet chariot,
> Coming fer to carry me home. . . .

Bigger refuses to sing along:

> Jan joined in and Bigger smiled derisively. Hell, that ain't the tune, he thought.
> "Come on, Bigger, and help us sing it," Jan said.
> "I can't sing," he said again. (77)

Bigger listens to Mary and Jan's effort to sing the Negro spiritual and realizes the words are right, but something in the rendition is wrong. Yet he cannot sing the song either.

Bigger's refusal to sing might be read as a means of resisting the liberal advances Jan and Mary offer. However, his ability to actually sing the spiritual would connect him with the cultural productions of black people—who, from Bigger's perspective, have no valuable commodities. This song, like Mrs. Thomas's earlier, alludes to the African American history of movement through space and transcendence of place, of which each has but a limited understanding. Thus, the potential power of the music is subverted. (Later, Ellison will exploit the tension suggested by the cultural disparity between black people and white liberals, captured by this scene in *Invisible Man*. Mary and Jan's request for Bigger to sing is echoed by a "broad" white man in the brotherhood who asks the protagonist to sing. Brother Jack tells him that the invisible man does not sing, but, of course, he does. He answers the request without music, but by performing a blues riff nevertheless: he exclaims, "He hit me in the face with a yard of chitterlings!" [304]. His performance evokes laughter born of both pleasure and pain.)

It is Mary who provokes the musical exchange in the car. She is heir to the liberal guilt embodied by the combination of her philanthropic parents—a blind mother and an entrepreneurial father. She urges Bigger to express himself in ways he is incapable of, particularly in her presence. Continually, Mary calls for Bigger to express his voice. And even after he has un-selfconsciously complied with her wishes, she calls attention to his behavior in a manner that arouses his resentment:

> "You know, for *three* hours you haven't said *yes* or *no*."
> She doubled up with laughter. He tightened with hate. Again she was looking inside of him and he did not like it. (80)

This observation bothers Bigger. As in the earlier conversations, Mary wants to compel him to speak. Here she sees through his "iron reserve," and Bigger is caught off guard. Essentially she is trying to affirm the significance of his unarticulated voice by urging him toward expression. The problem is that she thinks she knows what he has to express. Her rendition of the spiritual is characteristic of her presumptuousness. While Mary may know the words, she does not know the tune, familiarity with which comes from reconciling the words and melody with intimate knowledge of a cultural past not her own. On the other hand, Bigger might recognize both the tune and the lyrics, but he cannot sing.

Earlier that day, he had asked his mother across the breakfast table, "What you want me to do? Shout?" (15). In an ironic twist on shouting, an expression of religious (emotional) abandon, Bigger does shout, responding to Mary's call for voice. What he learns, however, is neither a dance nor a yell. It is murder masked as voice: "He had learned to shout and had shouted and no ear had heard him" (123). In part, Mary's ignorance of the "tune" she wants to sing and even the fact that her perspective on things might be wrong conspire in her death. Her good intentions cannot overcome centuries of racial history. Getting so drunk that she needs to be carried to her room places both Mary and Bigger in a compromising position that leads to her suffocation. It is only afterward, however, that Bigger realizes he has answered the question he posed to his mother. He shouts and finds a creative expression. While creative expressiveness is fundamental to establishing an African American sense of home, it is illogical to suggest that Bigger could use murder to locate a stable place. Instead, the dynamics enacted by this kind of expression intrude upon the making of a home.

The exhilaration of murder supplants the momentary satisfaction provided by distractions like the game of "playing white" with Gus. Now tools such as this game, which are only minimally cathartic for Bigger, lose their effectiveness altogether. His desire to do *something* has been fulfilled through his very significant act of murder, which makes all his other practices seem trivial. Not long afterward, Bigger goes out with his girlfriend, Bessie, to a bar. While they sit listening to the music playing, Bigger realizes:

> He knew that he should have asked her to dance, but the excitement that had hold of him would not let him. He was feeling different tonight from every other night; he did not need to dance and sing and clown over the floor in order to blot out a day and night of doing nothing. (133)

Bigger's altered perspective on dance mirrors his position on religion and alcohol; in his mind they are simply passive means of coping.

Despite his estrangement from the black community and its cultural practices, after the murder, Bigger retreats into the relative safety of the Southside. The black belt provides a cover of normalcy that at least temporarily masks his guilt. Beyond the superficial camouflage, however, the food, music, and lifestyle that so fascinated Mary and Jan offer little solace for Bigger. In fact, he is disdainful of both his mother and Bessie, who are so immersed in their own cultural practices. Clearly, he views them as the same kind of individual. Bigger consistently compares the crutches they utilize to sustain themselves: "The same deep realization he had had that morning at home at the breakfast table, while watching Vera and Buddy and his mother came back to him; only it was Bessie he was looking at now and seeing how blind she was" (131). They are weak in the same way; therefore, they are dangerous to Bigger in the same way. Bessie uses alcohol as an opiate; Mrs. Thomas practices her religion. Bigger feels these women threaten his ability to survive in the world as he makes it and as it makes him. In the end, he believes he *must* kill Bessie.

After coercing her into participating in his murder/kidnapping scheme, he is prepared to murder her in cold blood, too. When Bessie realizes that Bigger has actually murdered a white woman, she tells him, "If you killed *her* you'll kill *me*" (168). Her growing awareness appears as a blues idiom:

"Lord, don't let this happen to me! I ain't done nothing for this to come to me! I just work! I ain't had no happiness, no nothing. I just work. I'm black and I work and don't bother nobody. . . ."

"Go on," Bigger said, nodding his head affirmatively; he knew the truth of all she spoke without telling it. "Go on and see what that gets you." (170)

Bigger rejects the vernacular sentiment of Bessie's common, urban experience. She speaks of the blues, but he refuses to accept her expression as valuable.

Here again, Bessie and Mrs. Thomas's religion are conflated. Bessie's pleading could read as a prayer, but not one born of faith—the fundamental element of Christianity. Consequently, like Mrs. Thomas's songs, Bessie's expression is fundamentally not Christian. So while her pleas take the form of a prayer, they have the cadence and the sentiment of the blues. They become an urban blues performance for which Bigger is her audience. As John McCluskey explains, "Surprisingly, the lament of Bessie Mears, Bigger Thomas' girlfriend, is the statement which most closely parallels the blues tradition. Bessie's plea is the plea of a woman who has known only heartache and poverty. Though she remains thinly characterized, we can hear faint strains of Bessie Smith and Ma Rainey in her voice" (336). However, Bessie's blues pleadings only confirm Bigger's alienation: "Her words had made leap to consciousness in him a thousand details of her life which he had long known and they made him see that she was in no condition to be taken along and at the same time in no condition to be left behind" (216). So even while acknowledging the truth of Bessie's blues, he dismisses them as ineffectual: "Go on and see what that gets you" (170). It's not truth that Bigger seeks—it is change in the conditions that shape his life.

Because Bigger refuses to acknowledge the intrinsic value of Bessie's blues, he denies the kinship implicit among common folk. But his sense of place is intrinsically connected with his sense of race: "How easy it would be for him to hide if he had the whole city in which to move about! They keep us bottled up here like wild animals, he thought" (233). Bigger is afraid of what Bessie knows about him and the murder, and he is afraid of how that information could be used by the authorities who are hunting him. But when he dismisses Bessie's words as worthless, he rejects the potential shelter of the black belt—the place is bound with the people and the narratives that influence the way it operates. For a short while he is able to hide in abandoned buildings and travel unmolested: "He climbed through the window and walked to the street, turned northward, joining the people passing. No one recognized him" (232). But this relative freedom does not last. His confinement can be diagrammed on two levels: the discursive realm, which seemingly offers no liberatory modes of expression apart from murder; and geographical place, which offers only limited access to material resources. The reality of his confinement is revealed as he plots his escape within the constricted boundaries of the black city, held captive by a symbolic, white blizzard: "There were many empty buildings with black windows, like blind eyes, buildings like skeletons standing with snow on their bones in the winter winds" (163).

Until he kills Mary, Bigger feels he has no means to adequately vent his frustration because the expressive vehicles of his community do not satisfy him. Yet this feeling of estrangement motivates him to deny the murder, despite the fact that Bessie has already figured it out. The expressive modes already established within the community are not expedient and leave Bigger's sociopolitical dilemma unchanged. The other influence upon Bigger's worldview is the lack of genuine cohesiveness within the black community. He, a black man, has killed a white woman, and that reality alone prohibits Bigger from speaking openly. The myth of a unified black community is unraveled after his crime is discovered. Two residents of the Southside exchange:

> "Ef Ah knowed where tha' nigger wuz Ah'd turn im up 'n' git these white folks off me."
> "But, Jack, ever' nigger looks guilty t' white folks when somebody's done a crime." (73)

While white authorities hold the entire black belt under siege for the actions of one man, the black community is polarized by their ideals and fears. Bigger's act sets events in motion that distort everything but the fundamental fact of Mary's murder.

By the end of the novel, Bigger cannot help but view himself as connected with black people and ultimately satisfies himself by situating his actions outside a moral dichotomy of right and wrong. Finally, the morbid creativity of his first expressive gesture gives way to a blues ethos. Through this mediating lens, Bigger recognizes what on some level his attorney, Max, refuses to see: that his actions might be considered somehow "appropriate" and "natural" if agency is attributed to the individual parts of the system that limits black people. While Max labels that racist system co-conspirator in Bigger's crimes, he is unwilling to take that next step that would allow Bigger to justify his actions as somehow proper within that larger schema, housed within the entire framework of his crime. Max stops short of becoming a participant in the urban blues performance—a means of translating murder into creative expression—that helps Bigger, as black migrant, impose meaning upon his environment and gives significance to his tragic experiences. Max's response of shock and horror foreshadows Mr. Norton's response in *Invisible Man* to Trueblood's tale of rape and incest. The liberal sensibilities that allow them to enter into a discussion about race mask the true horror of racism and, further, their place within racist practices.

The media representation of Bigger's trial demonstrates the degree to which the state apparatus has been able to bring the Frankenstein's monster of the threatening black man to life. "It is this Bigger of the media," Griffin says—the black, oversexed animal—"who is pursued, captured, tried, and executed. The overwhelming state apparatus leaps to violence when it can no longer contain him through housing and discourse" (129). Yet it is this Bigger who has managed to become a creator in and of himself. By daring to step outside the parameters defined by his socioeconomic circumstances into a realm not just of fear but also of flight, Bigger has managed to transform energy and bring his own monster to life.[5] This creative energy leads ultimately to Bigger's own violent end, but he does achieve a moment of flight via that rebellion. Although Bigger is never able to remove himself from the constraints of race imposed by the larger society and his flight takes shape inside a collapsing circle, for a short time, he has been able to sustain a sense of liberty that grows out of a self-awareness that complicity would never permit him to know.

As with any carnivalesque inversion, however, the original balance of power remains intact. However frightening Bigger's defiance may have been, he, like the black rat in the opening scene, is perceived as the intruder; no matter how valid his position, no matter how powerful his cause, he will be hunted, caught, and slain. Bigger is moving within a dynamic system that has many ways of maintaining itself.[6] The space[7] he carves out cannot be read as a frontier, the unexplored expanse suggested by the seemingly empty space that allows him to look up at the airplane in the sky; it is instead a small part of the Daltons' basement where he plots his cover-up. Doreen Massey reads place as "a subset of the interactions which construe space, a local articulation within the wider whole"

(115). While "space" is generally conceived in larger terms than "place," Bigger creates a space for himself that is a subset of someone else's place—the Dalton household. For this reason, he is doubly confined. Bigger is homeless in the sense in which Baker uses the term "placeless," and his space is liberating insofar as the terms defined by his blues performance are still functional.

On the subject of music and dance in *Native Son*, John Mc-Cluskey states:

> As a Marxist, *however*, Wright could not unqualifiedly extol the power and vitality of folk culture, as Harold Cruse has pointed out. Thus, for Wright in his early analysis, though folk expression might help define a group, its insights could not suffice to guide Black people to power (and, presumably, guide Black artists to a searching social critique) within a broader political context. (334)

The character that Wright created in Bigger reflected the author's perspective. To Bigger, people like his mother, who want to sing and shout, and Bessie, who wants to drink and dance, are foolish because they do not see the uselessness of their own actions. Moreover, it is difficult for him to separate the family from the place they inhabit.

Bigger's reading of his mother and siblings signifies upon his reading of the apartment and vice versa. He himself reads as part of and in contrast to the interior landscape of the kitchenette. In setting Bigger beside Vera and his mother and then moving him outward into the increasingly larger geographical planes of the streets, the Daltons' house, and the black belt, Wright charts a schematic of urban territory upon which these power dynamics are enacted. The interplay of insider versus outsider is initiated by Bigger's name, which overtly states his claim to a space outside his family and this cramped apartment. It is not simply that Bigger is literally that, bigger than his family and this stultifying space they are forced to occupy. Rather, in the dialectical language of blues expressiveness that characterizes so much of Wright's ultimate worldview, Wright asserts that the nation is BIGGER—bigger than the man, bigger than the black belt, but, importantly, bigger than the Daltons and Buckley, too. Thus the largeness of the city is merely an illusion. In this dialectical framework, then, the black rat remains a threat and explodes the notion of home. Home is not reconciled with Bigger. And we find that Bigger is biggest—too big for the city, the kitchenette, or the Daltons' basement.

Notes

1. Richard Wright's *Native Son* (1940) is the literary forebear of Ralph Ellison's *Invisible Man* (1947). Perhaps no other African American authors have been more accepted into the traditional canon of American literature than these two men. Their masterpieces of fiction have become a standard part of a liberal arts curriculum. While we might find varied representations of both the city and home in the work of other male authors like Langston Hughes, Jean Toomer, and Alain Locke from the Harlem Renaissance era or more contemporary authors like James Baldwin, Ernest Gaines, and LeRoi Jones (Amiri Baraka), it seems prudent to spend some effort examining home as it is represented in these two works, which are so accepted. Not only do they speak directly to the issues of home within the context of African America, but they also inform the writings of those who follow. No major African American author since the publication of *Native Son* and *Invisible Man* is unaware of or unaffected by the novels' legacies.

2. Hurston's reading of shouting is distinctly secular. It serves well in this discussion of secular expressions like the blues, which is very often set in opposition to sacred practices of worship.

3. Until recent decades these churches, which are now the fastest growing Christian denominations in the world, had been classified as cults by sociologists like E. Franklin Frazier. They were looked upon with disdain by the black middle class. See *The Negro Church in America* (New York: Schocken Books, 1974).

4. The verse continues: *Watch the curves, the hills, the tunnels; never falter, never quail. Keep you hand upon the throttle and you eye upon the rail.*

5. Craig Werner notes the ways in which Wright utilizes a line from T. S. Eliot's "The Love Song of J. Alfred Prufrock"—"There will be time to murder and create"—which is based upon "the momentary exhilaration associated with Bigger's discovery of his own significance." *New Essays on Native Son* (New York: Cambridge University Press, 1970), 132.

6. In the manner described by Ross Chambers's *Room for Maneuver: Reading (the) Oppositional (in) Literature* (Chicago: University of Chicago Press, 1991), power structures are designed to permit a level of opposition: "Oppositional behavior consists of individual or group survival tactics that do not challenge power in place, but make use of circumstances set up by that power for purposes the power may ignore or deny. It contrasts, then, with revolution, which is a mode of *resistance* to forms of power it regards as illegitimate, that is, as a force that needs to be opposed by a counter force" (1). Toni Morrison's *Playing in the Dark: Whiteness and the Literary Imagination* (Cambridge: Harvard University Press, 1992) also describes such a systematic approach to resistance. As she writes about slave narratives, "Whatever popularity the slave narratives had—and they influenced abolitionists and converted anti-abolitionists—the slave's own narrative, while freeing the author in many ways, did not destroy the master narrative. The master narrative could make any number of adjustments to keep itself intact" (50–51).

7. Space and place work cooperatively. Generally, space is read as undefined or expansive while place is perceived as defined and therefore limited. Understanding one requires knowledge of the other because as spatial terms function, their oppositions gain their meaning when set one beside the other. See Michel de Certeau, *The Practice of Everyday Life* (Berkeley: University of California Press, 1984), 117–18. Here I use the term "space" rather than "place" because it connotes the freedom of movement Bigger has been denied by the tyranny of place.

Living (Just Enough) for the City: *Native Son* [37]

Works Cited

Baker, Houston A., Jr. *Blues, Ideology, and Afro-American Literature: A Vernacular Theory*. Chicago: University of Chicago Press, 1984.

——. "Richard Wright and the Dynamics of Place in Afro-American Literature." In Keneth Kinnamon, ed., *New Essays on Native Son*. New York: Cambridge University Press, 1970.

Ellison, Ralph. *Invisible Man*. New York: Vintage, 1947.

Giles, James. *The Naturalistic Inner-City Novel in America: Encounters with the Fat Man*. Columbia: University of South Carolina Press, 1995.

Gilyard, Keith. *Modern Critical Interpretations: Native Son*. Ed. Harold Bloom. Philadelphia: Chelsea House, 1988.

——. "The Sociolinguistics of Underground Blues." *Black American Literature Forum* 19 (4) (1985): 158–59.

Griffin, Farah Jasmine. *"Who Set You Flowin'?": The African-American Migration Narrative.* New York: Oxford University Press, 1995.

Harris, Trudier. "Native Sons and Foreign Daughters." In Keneth Kinnamon, ed., *New Essays on* Native Son. New York: Cambridge University Press, 1970.

Hurston, Zora Neale. *The Sanctified Church.* New York: Marlowe and Company, 1981.

Kinnamon, Keneth, ed. Introduction to *New Essays on* Native Son. New York: Cambridge University Press, 1970.

Massey, Doreen. "Double Articulation: A Place in the World." In Angelika Bammer, ed., *Displacements: Cultural Identities in Question.* Bloomington: Indiana University Press, 1994.

McCall, Dan. *The Example of Richard Wright.* New York: Harcourt, Brace and World, 1969.

McCluskey, John, Jr. "Two Steppin': Richard Wright's Encounter with Blues-Jazz." *American Literature* 55 (3) 1983: 332–44.

Reilly, John M. "Giving Bigger a Voice: The Politics of Narrative in *Native Son.*" In Keneth Kinamon, ed., *New Essays on* Native Son. New York: Cambridge University Press, 1970.

Wright, Richard. *Native Son.* New York: Bantam, 1940.

——. *12 Million Black Voices.* New York: Thunder's Mouth Press, 1941.

2

Keep on Moving Don't Stop:
Invisible Man

The title *Native Son* is clearly ironic; Bigger Thomas has no home or paternity. Yet the novel lays out three terms that sketch a blueprint for the place of home within African American literature traceable through works produced over the following three decades: the city,

Invisible Man was *par excellence* the literary extension of the blues. It was as if Ellison had taken an everyday twelve bar tune . . . and scored it for an orchestra.

—Albert Murray

When I had come to New York seven years before that, I wondered about the need for such huge buildings. No one ever seemed to be in them for very long; everyone was out on the sidewalks, moving, moving, moving—and to where?

—Gloria Naylor, *Mama Day*

the kitchen, and the womb. The city dominates Bigger's landscape even as he is pressed into geographically more restrictive spaces. The kitchen is represented as the kitchenette, an abbreviated version of a more complete place; and Bigger's retreat into the basement of the Dalton house is but the initial stage of a literary retreat into the womb.

In Ralph Ellison's masterpiece published twelve years later, *Invisible Man* (1952), the nameless protagonist goes on a journey that begins at the end, when he seems to have found "a home of sorts"—a basement apartment in an "all white" building outside Harlem. I will examine the ways that Ellison picks up and revises the theme of home that appears in *Native Son* specifically as the three geographical markers. I am interested in the changes Ellison makes in representing these sites so that they seem to yield the possibility of community fundamental to establishing home. The womb is defined more clearly in this novel, and the kitchen also plays a more significant role in *Invisible Man* than in *Native Son*. However, the city still dominates the landscape and serves as the chief concern in the narrator's quest for home.

Invisible Man augments the scenes of home found in *Native Son* as Ellison explores other possibilities of the Northern city. Numerous scenes, most within the city, provide the backdrop for the plot. Of all the settings featured in *Invisible Man*, Mary Rambo's house most reads as "home" because it contains her blues kitchen. In addition to Mary's house, only the basement apartment and the South are overtly characterized as home for the invisible man. The narrator looks over his shoulder to the South, a place to which he will never return. For a time, it guides his movements as Kansas does Dorothy's on her journey through Oz. The basement is a more overt representation of the womb than Bigger's basement in *Native Son*. In contrast to the city, which resists being configured as home, Mary's house, with its blues kitchen, and the basement apartment, a womblike place, lend themselves to being read as home. Yet something remains in place to trouble such a reading. We imagine home to be stable and therefore stabilizing, but Ellison builds upon Wright's problematization of stability as a quality of home. The impermeability of Wright's city does not prove stabilizing, despite the fact that it remains static. In contrast, Ellison focuses on the changing face of the city that refuses to be known or knowable, and thus refuses to engender the familiarity fundamental to the construct of home.

As in *Native Son*, in this novel the blues seems to be part and parcel of the black (home) place. Unlike Wright, Ellison believed music was a vital aspect of his literary aesthetic. Instead of social protest, Ellison sought to create art; and his art would be infused with the movement and cadence of the blues. Berndt Ostendorf says:

> Vernacular dance, vernacular language, and vernacular music represent for this high cultural modernist a total body of culture. And Ellison wants to translate that energy into the organized discipline of his art. . . . Jazz, dance, and language all partake of a total world view and a total way of life. Hence, one of the harshest estimates that Ellison ever made of Richard Wright was that "he knew very little about jazz and didn't even know how to dance." (97)

Wright's inability to dance is tantamount to Bigger's inability to sing. Stereotypically, "Black folk got rhythm," if they do not have anything else. Ellison, believing that music and dance are fundamental to African American culture, suggests that for a black man, not knowing how to dance means lacking a crucial foundation. It is through understanding of these cultural practices that black people become connected with one another. Although the blues cannot mitigate all of the debilitating effects experienced at home, it provides a cadence through which some of the occupants make a culture of privation more bearable.

Womb: The Truebloods' Cabin

By the second chapter of the novel, two of the three terms have been introduced. The narrator, in the prologue, is already underground in New York City. But the novel goes back to the time when his journey began in the South. The Trueblood episode appears in the second chapter of *Invisible Man*. Jim Trueblood is a sharecropper who lives with his family near the campus of the college the narrator attends briefly. The narrator inadvertently escorts Mr. Norton, a wealthy white trustee, to the Truebloods' cabin. Initially Mr. Norton is struck by the age and style of the structure: "It was an old cabin with its chinks filled with chalk-white clay, with bright new shingles patching its roof" (46). He notices the cabins first, then, "looking across the bare, hard stretch of yard . . . two women dressed in new blue-and-white checked ginghams," both of whom "moved with the weary, full-fronted motions of far-gone pregnancy" (47). Filled with wonder that the buildings have lasted since slavery, Mr. Norton exclaims, "The human stock goes on, even though it degenerates. But these cabins!" (47). Mr. Norton expects the "human stock" to continue despite its degeneration but he is full of wide-eyed amazement that the man-made cabins endure so well. From his perspective, the pregnant black woman is part of an old scene of the black South. These structures and the women working in the yard, he intimates, are enduring evidence of a more wholesome past.

The narrator is mortified by his own impropriety, having stumbled upon the Truebloods without forethought. Jim Trueblood is a disgrace to the local black community, particularly the petit bourgeoisie at the college. He has brought shame to everyone by impregnating both his wife, Kate, and his eldest daughter, Matty Lou. These are the two women dressed alike and bearing the weight of pregnancy, like twins, working together in the yard. In introducing Mr. Norton to Jim Trueblood, the narrator discloses the dark underbelly of the poverty of black domestic life. The pregnant womb is necessarily part of this construction because, as even Mr. Norton recognizes in his pejorative understanding of African Americans, home is built around family. Patriarchy relies upon the woman as the kin source, and men operating under this philosophy look to women to bring forth the next generation. While no home place can be constructed around gender without some inherent conflict, the terrain of the black (home) place of the sharecropper pictured here is made even more treacherous by poverty, racism, and the imbalance of power between the genders.

Mr. Norton is attracted to the Truebloods' tale as if by a force beyond his control. He demands that the narrator stop and let him speak to Trueblood himself. Trueblood willingly narrates his woeful tale to the Northern, white, liberal philanthropist. Unable to afford coal, the family conserves body heat by sleeping together in two pallets on the floor. The younger children are in one and Matty Lou between her parents in the other. Trueblood recounts his thoughts, which include reminiscing about a past love and fending off a current suitor interested in Matty Lou, but he places responsibility for his behavior on a "dream-sin": he awakened from a dream to discover he was having intercourse with his daughter.

Initially, Ellison describes the setting as "dark, plum black. Black as the middle of a bucket of tar" (54). In this black place, he lays out the dynamics of home at work in this novel. The Truebloods' log cabin is a remnant of slavery. This part of the material landscape has hardly been altered since prior to the Civil War. This black (home) place that began in racist Southern oppression and poverty ends in the same shack with a mother and daughter impregnated by the same man. Although Mr. Norton hardly can be credited with recognizing the nuances of these sophisticated racial dynamics, he is correct in that, indeed, one incestuous seed "degenerates." Kate and Matty Lou bear the tragedy of home literally in their bodies. The two pregnant women, mother and daughter, signify the privation out of which Trueblood's blues are created.

At first, the narrator is baffled by his confrontation with Trueblood, but the sharecropper contributes one of the most profound lessons the unnamed protagonist receives in his long journey. Trueblood's blues are characterized by John S. Wright as the "creative will to transcendence" (176). Upon awakening from his nightmarish dream and recognizing his quagmire (that he is having intercourse with his daughter while his wife is lying next to them in bed), Trueblood explains, "Once a man gits hisself into a tight spot like that there ain't much he can do. It ain't up to him no longer. There I was, tryin' to git away with all my might, yet having to move without movin'. I flew in but I had to walk out. I had to move without movin'" (59). Trueblood is caught within a situation that inflicts terrible pain upon himself as well as his family; at the same moment he experiences pleasure great enough to create an unresolvable predicament. Movement is both the problem and the solution. The narrator himself will come to accept Trueblood's quintessential blues paradox: having to arrive at the result without ever performing the action. As John S. Wright explains, "In his full awareness, then, of the irredeemable cost of freedom from sin and the attendant consequences of freely sinning, Trueblood gives eloquent testimony to his own tragic sense of life and to that need for transcendence he finally satisfies only in the resolving poetry of the blues" (176).

Incest is not the shocking new ground Mr. Norton discovers that hot afternoon as he listens to the tale. Instead, he ventures into "new territory" when he stumbles upon Trueblood's yard and encounters the black (home) place and the blues. What confounds him even more than the fact of incest is the fact that Jim Trueblood seems to have escaped judgment: "You did and are unharmed!" (51). It seems Trueblood has found a resolution to his personal dilemma. He *can* move without moving, as Norton demonstrates by rewarding his performance. Along with so many other guilt-ridden, wealthy white men, Norton is moved by Trueblood's tale while Trueblood, as blues performer, does not have to *move* at all.

The sharecropper's home, which had been threatened by poverty, the mock charity of Northern liberals, and the racial pragmatism of the black college, is now maintained by Jim Trueblood's retellings of his story. He transforms his own painful experience into a blues performance. Already known for his singing and storytelling, Trueblood has polished his tale, reconfiguring tragic circumstances to make his life more livable. His family is clad in new clothing, his roof patched with new shingles bought with money garnered from patrons of his art. Trueblood is an agent of the blues. In contrast, the women are not heard. The mark left on Jim's face from Kate's swing of an ax is the sole evidence of her resistance. Matty Lou is just silenced; she "won't speak a word to nobody" (67).

Rape is a high price for Matty Lou to pay in order for her father to be rewarded as an agent of the blues. And as Ann du Cille, Hortense Spillers, and other African American feminist critics have emphasized, care must be taken not to reduce her to an object of patriarchy.[1] She does not get to narrate her own tale; that authority is given (quite naturally) to her father, who, even after violating the (natural) rights of his daughter, retains his domestic dominance (as evidenced by the failure of his wife's attempt to kill him). To deny the horror of the scene and only acknowledge the blues expression that emerges from it risks, as Ann du Cille suggests in a critique of Houston Baker's reading of the episode, reducing race to rape. Rape is the means through which Trueblood gains his power, at the expense of Kate and, most notably, Matty Lou. His role as father is doubly confirmed by the two pregnant women. In this household, as opposed to that of Bigger Thomas, paternity is clear—all too clear.

Kitchen: Mary Rambo's Blues Kitchen

While Bigger is unable to discover a safe place to roost in the course of his desperate flight, that is precisely what the invisible man unwittingly finds in Mary Rambo's house. The novel actually begins "underground," in the basement of an apartment in New York City, as the invisible man recites the story of how his journey to that point began. He has been propelled from place to place by a series of events that makes it impossible for him to have the comfort of a stable home. After arriving in New York, he must come to understand the naïveté of the hope that he will be allowed to return to the deep South (somehow improved by his experiences). Still reeling from yet another sudden shift in place, the narrator emerges from a subway and finds himself ushered into Mary Rambo's house.

Mary meets the visibly ailing narrator on the street, and with some assistance from another passerby, helps him into her home. This house, more than any other in the novel, manifests the mythic possibilities of home that must be constructed, at least partially, around the familiarity fostered by the past. Yet it too is part of urban blues culture and reflects the tension of blues vernacular. The blues speak of a dialectic created in the opposition of privation, poverty, and racism with privilege, wealth, and liberty. Mary's position as caregiver is well known within the community, and she expects the residents to be familiar with her reputation. She reassures the ailing protagonist, *"You take it easy, I'll take care of you like I done a heap of others, my name's Mary Rambo, everybody knows me round this part of Harlem"* (252). Mary ushers the protagonist into his next venue as she compels him to take refuge in her home.

Mary allows him to reside in her house without fear of eviction or of the social elitism that is so pervasive at the Men's House—from which he has just been banished for pouring a spittoon over the head of a reverend, whom he has mistaken for Dr. Bledsoe. Bledsoe is the Southern administrator who betrayed him by sending him to work in New York in the futile hope of returning to school. At Mary's house, he finds the comfort of good company, rest, and food. He explains his relationship with her in this way, "Other than Mary I had no friends and desired none. Nor did I think of Mary as a 'friend': she was something more—a force, a stable, familiar force like something out of my past which kept me from whirling off into some unknown which I dared not face" (258).

Friends have become obsolete in the narrator's world after Bledsoe's betrayal. Mary does not serve as "friend"; rather, she is an anchor of sorts that rescues him from an unfamiliar, and therefore terrifying, abyss of urban Northern life. The greater the "unknown," the more familiar and stabilizing is Mary. The "unknown" that the narrator so fears is not an identifiable place. Instead, it is an expanse of unencoded space that would consume him, were it not for the grounding Mary provides. The expanse feels threatening when set within the context of Harlem, the city that refuses to be constant for the invisible man. Mary's house offers the consolation of a definite site sheltered from the city, which only exacerbates the perceived chaos.

The expanse of the Northern city had seduced the protagonist and left him sick and stumbling up from the subway. Mary's "familiarity" contrasts with this large strangeness. But the narrator has difficulty articulating Mary's relationship to him. Like music, she is beyond words. Her house becomes "the South right in the middle of Manhattan" that Farah Griffin describes in *"Who Set you Flowin'?" The African American Migration Narrative*. Like the atmosphere created by the blues performance Griffin describes, Mary embodies not the South so much as "home." She becomes a meta-place that exists as a locale in the abstract. As such, Mary suggests the familiarity of Southern ritual culture without actually material-izing the South. In her house, the narrator is able to find the solace of Southern practices without leaving town. She opens her doors selflessly to this man who could be categorized as a "stranger." The dichotomies inherent in the construct of home, which operate to make Mary recognizable inside the strangeness of the city, con-versely function to make the protagonist known, or at least not a stranger, to her. In this way Mary and her guest develop a relation-ship that is not contingent upon knowing the personal details of each other's life. Mary is familiar to him because of the cultural val-ues she represents; consequently, her house reads as "home." The blues performance that makes "the South right in the middle of Manhattan" is a musical configuration. Hence, Mary is reconfig-ured in this way as well.

The musical value system she embodies is made up of blue notes that begin with a man sick and stumbling into the arms of a care-taker. The narrator explains, "When I came out of the subway, Lenox Avenue seemed to career away from me at a drunken angle, and I focused upon the teetering scene with wild, infant's eyes, my head throbbing" (251). Here again the underground is a womblike place. Coming out of the subway station is like being reborn and given to a new mother. Mary shelters the narrator without concern for how his presence might impact her own well-being. When she is low on food and money, she serves cabbage instead of complain-ing or refusing to feed someone. What she demands in return ap-pears as a benign pressure to perform "some act of leadership, some noteworthy achievement" (258).

The underlying tension in Mary's house is reflected by this pres-sure and the cabbage—suggesting the permeability of home and its potential to be infiltrated by larger forces like economics associated with maintaining such places. In another sense, the circumstances at Mary's house demonstrate the flexibility of the blues. Within the context of the blues, strangers can be allied unproblematically with each other, as are Mary and the protagonist. Further, the blues creates a space where circumstances like poverty can be integrated into the structure of home, Mary's house, without complete ruin.[2] While contemplating the meaning of the cabbage and the pressure in his room, the narrator hears Mary in the kitchen: "Then from down the hall I could hear Mary singing, her voice clear and untroubled, though she sang a troubled song. It was the 'Back Water Blues.' I lay listening as the sound flowed to and around me, bringing me a calm sense of my indebtedness" (297).

The blues serves Mary as a repository into which she can pour her pain and negative emotion. Mary's blues kitchen emerges as part of a larger cultural practice of establishing "home ground." The blues becomes a metaphorical bottle tree that is constructed to guard the home and protect its occupants by containing the evil.[3] Mary's blues, in effect, seeks to capture the evil "spirit" that troubles her home. The blues kitchen helps her negotiate the conflict between her home as a safe space and poverty as a threat to that perceived serenity—and the song brings order and meaning to her guest's experience.

The narrator's sense of indebtedness to Mary motivates the invisible man to accept a job with a political organization known as the Brotherhood so that he can repay her. Ironically, this job requires him to move. On his last day at Mary's home, the invisible man is awakened by a jarring sound. The cacophony has a very different effect on him than the blues tones of Mary's kitchen. The disembodied sound of metal striking against the metal of the radiator pipes reverberates throughout the building and infuriates the protagonist. He expresses hostility toward the people behind this commotion by looking for a weapon with which to contribute his own noisy blows to the pipe:

> Then near the door I saw something which I'd never noticed there before: the cast-iron figure of a very black, red-lipped and wide-mouthed Negro, whose white eyes stared up at me before his chest. It was a bank, a piece of early Americana, the kind of bank which, if a coin is placed in the hand a lever pressed upon the back, will raise its arm and flip the

coin into the grinning mouth. For a second I stopped, grabbed it, suddenly as enraged by the tolerance or lack of discrimination, or whatever, that allowed Mary to keep such a self-mocking image around, as by the knocking. (319)

Mary wonders at the racket caused by the numerous tenants throughout the building, and her bewilderment is expressed in her characteristic blues idiom, "They know when the heat don't come up that the super's drunk or done walked off the job looking for his woman, or something. Why don't folks act according to what they know?" (320). This kind of expressiveness is what allows the potential for pleasure to coexist with the likelihood of pain, and contrasts with the narrator's cacophony. Her vernacular gives voice to the rage that he so vehemently desires to articulate through his attack upon the pipe. It seems appropriate to him to use the bank that he finds so offensive. But Mary is puzzled by the self-centeredness of a response that focuses on one's own feelings of discomfort rather than recognizing the interconnectedness of human beings in the struggle to endure.

Mary identifies with the super's position as another expression of need, akin to her own. She has the unusual ability to recognize and, further, to validate another person's pain. This is significant precisely because it is a difficult thing to do, as Elaine Scarry describes:

> For the person in pain, so incontestably and unnegotiably present is it that "having pain" may come to be thought of as the most vibrant example of what it is to "have certainty," while for the other person it is so elusive that "hearing about pain" may exist as the primary model of what it is "to have doubt." Thus pain comes unsharably into our midst as at once that which cannot be denied and that which cannot be confirmed. (4)

Mary bridges the chasm between the certainty embodied by her own experience of pain and the doubt about another's. Through her blues vernacular, she correlates her own experiences with the actions of those around her (even as their actions further inconvenience her), incorporating new circumstances into her blues vocabulary as they arise. In contrast, the narrator cannot handle the disruption and has trouble identifying with the figure that he finds so offensive. Yet he is able to note the pain in the bank's expression, which "seemed more of a strangulation than a grin" (312). The bank's visage shows the classic paradox of blues expressiveness that balances between pain and pleasure. This face both "grins and lies" in the way that Paul Laurence Dunbar describes in his poem "We Wear the Mask":

We wear the mask that grins and lies,
It hides our cheeks and shades our eyes,—
This debt we pay to human guile;
With torn and bleeding hearts we smile,
And mouth with myriad subtleties.

The "subtleties" of the expression are key to understanding a complex history.

Mask wearing is inseparable from the African American historical experience; no amount of shame or anger can erase the past. African Americans have been forced to contort their sorrow into laughter, anger into a grin. As Wright states in *12 Million Black Voices*, "The ridiculousness and sublimity of love are captured in our blues, those sad-happy songs that laugh and weep in one breath, those mocking tender utterances of a folk imprisoned in steel and stone" (128). The "steel and stone" framework of the city promotes the contradictory impulses that began centuries earlier, in the Middle Passage, the smiling through tears. The bank is a blues artifact that could anchor the invisible man's profound history of pain, resistance, fortitude, and pride. Yet the narrator is so angry about the stereotype it represents that he refuses to identify with the pain inherent in its expression.

He quickly dismisses the observations that might help him identify with the hidden pain (and Scarry suggests that pain is always concealed if it is not experienced personally); hence, he misses the lessons that might be learned by empathizing with others and sharing their grief. As Griffin notes, his judgment is impaired by his inability to comprehend the multifaceted layers of his experiences:

This question, "What does it mean?" is Invisible Man's constant refrain. He is ambitious and somewhat pretentious. He feels that in order to reach his goal of leadership, he must shun those elements that bind him to a racial past. While he seeks to lead black people, it is an empty aspiration that fails to recognize the value of racial wisdom. Nowhere is this contradiction more evident than in his relationship with Mary. (131)

For the narrator to empathize with and share the grief expressed by the bank, he would have to be willing to ally himself with the collectivity the figure represents. The blues ethos that permits this kind of identification is, after all, a vernacular expression. But he is not yet ready to make the conscious choice to identify with this segment of his racial community. He dismisses his observation of the "strangulation" and the awareness it might bring. Instead, he uses the bank as a weapon to unleash his anger upon the unseen forces. Not surprisingly, in the process he smashes the head apart; and that which he hoped to destroy, he will not be permitted to discard.

City: Dispossession

Ellison assigns value to Mary's house by juxtaposing it with a scene of an eviction (one potential effect of that "unknown" space that the narrator fears) involving an old black couple. The narrator uses Mary as the point of contrast by which he assigns meaning to the city. The metropolis is large; Mary is small. While her house is not large enough to accommodate the invisible man's needs, she is an invaluable resource for him as he comes to understand his place within the urban territory.

Like the sense of homelessness found in *Native Son*, dispossession illustrates the relationship certain people have with the places they occupy. At the first eviction the narrator has ever witnessed, he makes an impassioned speech in an attempt to subdue an angry crowd, trying to explain the meaning of "dispossession." He expounds:

"'Dispossess,' eighty-seven years and dispossessed of what? They ain't *got* nothing, they can't *get* nothing, they never *had* nothing. So who was dispossessed?" I growled. "We're law abiding. So who's being dispossessed? Can it be us? These old ones are out in the snow, but we're here with them. Look at their stuff, not a pit to hiss in, nor a window to shout the news and us right with them. Look at them, not a shack to pray in or an alley to sing the blues! (279)

After eighty-seven years, the elderly couple has little of material value, and their condition presages the state of the entire community. Ellison draws upon William Faulkner's use of the dispossession theme in *Go Down, Moses,* where Ike struggles with the idea when he inherits land because the rightful heir, Lucas Beauchamp, is black. Ike dispossesses his cousin, Lucas, of the land (only to repudiate it later). Ike laments, "Dispossessed of Eden. Dispossessed of Canaan, and those who dispossessed him dispossessed him dispossessed" (247). Ellison recasts this literary theme from Faulkner's Mississippi within the setting of the Northern city. Dispossession is an active condition enforced upon the community by officials with orders such as those who block the old couple's door. The narrator captures in his speech the sense of transience and indeterminacy that residents, recast as travelers, experience in city life.

When we meet the invisible man in the prologue, he has taken up residence in the basement of an apartment building. He has lit it with 1,369 light bulbs illuminated by unregulated electricity. The protagonist uses the lights to establish this territory as his home. Marking territory in this way can be situated within the African American practice of establishing "home ground." Anthropologist Grey Gundaker claims that such practices exist within the context of African America from coast to coast in both urban and rural settings: "Scale varies, but the claim, I am here, stays the same" (1). In this gesture, the narrator declares, "I am here," but with much less emphasis on the "here" than on the "I am." One reason is that place, within the context of the novel, continues to be unstable, as tenuous a construct as any seemingly fixed identity.

In fact, Monopolated Light & Power, the electric company responsible for distribution of current for the area, believes that "a lot of free current is disappearing somewhere into the jungle of Harlem" (5). The power company is, of course, a faceless white corporation whose primary goal is to serve its own interests (which may overlap with the interests of the larger white community), presumably without considering the interests of the black community. The company is quick to place blame for the loss of current on the African American community. Harlem is a black place. It is indisputably the section of New York City reserved for African Americans, so the reference to it as a "jungle" carries racist connotations. Harlem is read here as a barbaric wilderness, an untamed expanse that is far too frightening and free to be conquered. From the white perspective represented by ML&P, at best such a place can only be contained.

The invisible man exploits the image of Harlem as jungle to avoid the possibility of being discovered. Harlem during the 1920s was the scene of a great rebirth of African American culture; the contemporary Harlem pictured here contrasts with the image of that era.[4] The protagonist explains, "The joke, of course, is that I don't live in Harlem" (5). This is part of the irony. ML&P's expectation that a power drainage must come from inside the "jungle" is so restrictive that no one with this perspective could imagine that the drainage is coming from elsewhere—let alone an "all white" building *outside* of Harlem. Yet the lines delineating Harlem from the rest of Manhattan are more permeable than ML&P wishes to admit. As Gloria Anzaldúa writes, "Borders are set up to define the places that are safe and unsafe, to distinguish *us* from *them*. A border is a dividing line, a narrow strip along a steep edge. A borderland is a vague and undetermined place created by the emotional residue of an unnatural boundary. It is in a constant state of transition" (3). Borders, as Anzaldúa defines them, are a type of threshold that is constantly in flux. In the prologue, the invisible man has made this basement into a borderland home of sorts. If he embraces the border as his home, we might expect that he is also embracing the idea of change and mixtures. The despotism of one culture over another, of the power company's monopoly over Harlem, is challenged by the metaphor of in-betweenness. So the invisible man finds comfort in this retreat: "The point now is that I found a home—or a hole in the ground, as you will" (5).

The basement hideaway may be read as a transitional space between what is characterized as the "jungle"—representing the African American ghetto—and civilization, the white city. According to the logic employed by ML&P, a black man should not reside outside the "jungle" of Harlem and no white person in this apartment building would be siphoning electricity. But having recently come to the awareness that his identity is more precisely fixed as an *invisible* man than a *black* man, the narrator is able to orchestrate this ruse and manipulate the power structure into deceiving itself. He manages this scam because of society's insistence upon classifying places as well as people in the ways that Anzaldúa illuminates—according to race, gender, nationality, etc. It is important to ML&P and the culture associated with the corporation to be able to delineate its boundaries of power in order to maneuver the opposition (either real or imagined) onto a plane that operates under its authority. As Doreen Massey articulates:

> Two points seem clear. First, and very obviously, the way in which we characterize places is fundamentally political. But second, and far less obviously perhaps, the politics lie not just in the particular characteristics assigned to places (whether they include racist or sexist features, to which social class they are assigned) but in the very way in which the image of place is constructed. (114)

The division that demarcates the jungle and separates it from the rest of the city draws a line of safety with which the white community is able to assuage their fears of an African American threat. Identifying the territory of the jungle and African Americans as its occupants allows the whites to blindly insist upon the truth of its boundaries.

Perhaps the narrator turns on 1,369 bulbs in order to shed light on the intangibility of the barriers between the races. He then contradicts the authority of these boundaries through his tale. The reader, aware from the prologue of the narrator's true location, is not deceived by the apartment building's claim of being "all white." Hegemony's borders are not hard and fast. Instead it is the very permeability of those delineations that allows the structure to endure.

By the time the invisible man has gone through the Brotherhood and encountered Todd Clifton and Ras the Destroyer, he has come to accept the movement that compels him from place to place as a part of the African American collective condition. As he is moved, he is forced to receive both material and psychological signs that connect him to the collective experience. His briefcase is now full of indicators of his travels, and he has the potential to identify himself as part of a larger community of racialized people and sites. But that community still refuses to yield itself to the invisible man's needs. The Harlem riot is one of the last venues depicted in the novel. During the riot the illusion of stability ordinarily associated with place gives way to chaos. In the midst of this extreme disorder, the narrator again longs for home.

The portrait of Mary surfaces as a maternal, stable, and ordering figure that comes to be read overtly as home: "It was not a decision of thought but something I realized suddenly while running over puddles of milk in the black street, stopping to swing the heavy brief case and the leg chain, slipping and sliding out of their hands" (551). Those signs of his journey—the case heavy with the weight of the coins, the bank he broke at Mary's house, and the leg chain given to him earlier by Tarp—become the physical manifestations of the vernacular blues expressiveness inherent in black experiences, which have the potential to defend him against hostile enemies. Although the physical weight of the metal blues artifacts protects him during the upheaval of the riot, like Bigger in his doomed flight, the narrator is searching for a safe place to roost. He is trying to reach Mary's house, but he is running the wrong way. He cannot go back to Mary's—the maternal imagery is rendered useless as the milk already wasted upon the ground.

The past is not available to the protagonist because of the laws of physics, regardless of social, cultural, or personal history. Further, as Doreen Massey suggests, "There is no one essential past about which to get nostalgic. This is true in the sense that there has never been a historical movement untouched by the world beyond" (116). Time is the inevitably corrupting presence that complicates the ability to construct home as an ideal in the present. The knowledge required to construct home as a perfected shelter is predicated upon experience that comes through living over time. The invisible man cannot go home to Mary's because of the impossibility of returning through time and space with the knowledge he has acquired through the act of moving away. He is, indeed, moving in the wrong direction if he is trying to go home, because Mary's house becomes home for him only after he leaves. The challenge facing the invisible man is to use the tools available to him to create a home in the present. In the midst of this confusion, he suddenly finds himself falling to safety underground.

Womb: "A Home of Sorts" in the City

The narrator finds himself below ground after falling through an open manhole: "I was never to reach Mary's, and I was over-optimistic about removing the steel cap in the morning. . . . I tried to find the usual ladder that leads out of such holes, but there was none" (567). Falling underground, into a womblike place, in effect represents an impossible return. The serendipitous event parallels the desire to deliberately return to an originary moment while drawing upon the knowledge accumulated in his journey away from that very place. The narrator is able to use the things he has carried with him from his past as fuel. He burns the combustible objects in his briefcase in order to light his way out of the hole. Just as the leg chain and bank became pragmatic tools for his survival, these other things literally are able to help him survive.[5] This moment represents the culmination of past events as he tries to create a livable future out of the tools he has acquired.

The characterization of a place is, as Massey argues, "fundamentally political" because it is how societal institutions are able to sustain control over areas that otherwise would not belong to them. Although the characterizations may be presented as "natural," or unchanging essences already determined by the very existence of particular locations, they are dynamic rather than fixed. Consequently, Harlem is read as "jungle," not to determine accurately who is illegally pilfering power from ML&P, but to maintain the illusion of definitive boundaries and therefore the semblance of absolute control through the metaphor of containment. "Very often," Massey writes, "moreover, that intrinsic nature [of place] is seen as eternal, unchanging. And even where change is acknowledged, this approach often views the 'essence of place' as having evolved through a history which is read as a sense, an internal history" (11). If the narrator is African American and he lives outside the "jungle," then he challenges the logic embodied in the establishment of boundaries. However, it is the narrator's claim to invisibility that sets the ruse into action.

Motion is, of course, the primary directive of the novel: "Keep that nigger boy running." This directive sets the narrator in motion. Jerry Gafio Watts quotes Albert Murray saying, "'Improvisation,' Murray tells us 'is the ultimate human (i.e. heroic) endowment.' The blues-oriented hero is a matter of improvisation" (58). The narrator is such a blues hero, although the characterization is conflicted. By the end of the novel, he is claiming, "I would have to move them [Harlem] without myself being moved" (507). This sentiment echoes one he heard earlier from Jim Trueblood—"I had to move without movin'" (59). The narrator returns to that sentiment, derived from Trueblood's immoral rape and impregnation of his daughter alongside the legitimate impregnation of his wife. He tries to employ the sharecropper's blues logic in the environment of the ever-changing city. But the narrator cannot perform his way out of the blues paradox of the Harlem riot. His world has become one of sight, not invisibility, which illuminates rather than obscures the mechanisms that operate to maintain place. So Trueblood's solution to his perverse situation is thwarted in the narrator's relationship to Harlem. He cannot employ the blues strategy, so he is both physically and emotionally moved.

Another aspect of the home life captured in this revision of Trueblood's blues must not be overlooked. Jim Trueblood's blues reappear in the language of the protagonist, sanitized of the female body, that reminds us of the high stakes involved in blues production. Kate and Matty Lou are not accommodated by the narrator's blues sentiment, or more precisely, they are used and discarded. The black (home) place is subsumed within the more attractive figure of the pregnant black woman even as the woman is effaced by her womb. The slave cabin does not endure in the narrator's revision of Trueblood's blues—it has fallen away during the migration to the Northern city—and the "human stock . . . degenerates." From the outset, the narrator has been trying to get home—first back to the South, then to Mary's—and finally he finds himself underground. "I was in strange territory now and someone, for some reason, had removed the manhole cover and I felt myself plunge down, down . . . and I lay in the black dark . . . no longer running, hiding or concerned" (565). The womb reappears as a *man*hole, in Baker's terminology, "an irresistible attractive force" drawing all things into itself. This is indeed a black hole: "I tried to reach above me but found only space, unbroken and impenetrable" (567).

It would be nearly twenty years before Toni Morrison offered another vantage from which to view this impoverished black (home) place and its impact upon family life by introducing Pecola Breedlove in *The Bluest Eye*. In *Inspiriting Influences*, Michael Awkward reads Pecola, who suffers rape by her father, as a feminist revision of Matty Lou. I will discuss Pecola and the relationship incest has to the place of home further in the next chapter. The external specter of the city that haunts the migrants' early encounters in Wright's and Ellison's works is not the focus for Morrison in *The Bluest Eye*. While the male authors choose to focus on the confrontation between races that implicates the city, paying little deliberate attention to gender, home for this female author tends to read more specifically as the built physical structure. Yet, even as Morrison looks to the dynamics of a more intimate sphere, she records evidence of a devastating conflict that has the potential to destroy the quality of her characters' lives. The protagonist is threatened by directives issued from home that characterize human action and behavior as either legitimate or illegitimate. The city seems to fall away as we move further inside the built structure of home. Kitchens become the focal point in *The Bluest Eye*, before we again are pulled tragically into the womb.

Notes

1. Baker's reading of this scene in *Blues Ideology* ignited a firestorm among African American feminist critics because he suggests:

Only the Trueblood encounter reveals the phallus as producing Afro-American generations rather than wasting its seed upon the water. The cosmic force of the phallus thus becomes, in the ritual action of the Trueblood episode, symbolic of a type of royal paternity, an aristocratic procreativity turned inward to ensure the royalty (the "truth," "legitimacy," or "authenticity") of an enduring black line of descent (183).

Baker arges that Trueblood's union with his daughter produces a royal lineage, and thus Matty Lou becomes the source who ensures a black line through the act of rape by her own father. The phallus is supreme and compassion for the daughter is sublimated by the dominance of patrimony.

2. John Bardi of Pennsylvania State University, Mont Alto, performed a witty, philosophical interpretation of three musical forms at the "Blues Traditions: Memory, Criticism, and Pedagogy" conference at Pennsylvania State University in June 2000. His performance on electric guitar read music as a metaphor for political systems. He presented a baroque piece as "exclusive"—any notes from outside the classical scale are banished from the "kingdom" by the resolution of the piece. An avant-garde piece represented a chaotic and unstable government, while the blues successfully presented a system that afforded both order and inclusiveness.

3. Such practices can be seen throughout the American landscape as African Americans lay claim to the territory and structures they inhabit. Containers like gourds, jugs, and bottles are often hung from trees or set on porches near doorways to both guard and mark the home. The blues is another such container. Like the bottle trees that appear as a distinctly African American aesthetic practice, the blues plays a significant role in maintaining Mary's home ground. Robert Farris Thompson explains such cultural practices in "Bighearted Power: Kongo Presence in the Landscape and Art of Black America" (in Grey Gundarker, ed., *Keep Your Head to the*

Sky: Interpreting African American Home Ground [Charlottesville: University Press of Virginia, 1998]):

The *nkisi* tradition, brought to the United States from Kongo and Angola by Gullah Jack and other legendary healers, was a matter of embedding spirits in earths, keeping the spirit in a container to concentrate its power, and including with these earths material signs which told the spirit what to do. The gist of those expressions are seemingly regained in a creole art wherein the house guards the spirit of the owner and the icons in the yard guard or enhance that spirit with gestures of protection and enrichment.

A collection of *minkinsi* figures were featured in an exhibition at the Smithsonian as an introduction to a show featuring art by sculptor Renee Stout. At the entrance to the exhibition were these figures and a prominent sign explaining their presence and significance. The sign explained that the English language has no direct parallel for the word *"minkinsi." "Minkinsi* are fabricated things, yet they can be invoked to produce desired effects, they have a will of their own, and they may willfully command the behavior of human beings . . . people depend on *minkinsi* to do things for them, even to make life itself possible" (quoted in Wyatt Macaffey and Michael D. Harris, *Astonishment and Power: The Eyes of Understanding and the Art of Renee Stout* [Washington, D.C.: The Smithsonian Institution Press, 1993], 13).

4. For a comprehensive examination of the image of Harlem in literature see James De Jongh, *Vicious Modernism: Black Harlem and the Literary Imagination* (Cambridge: Cambridge University Press, 1990).

5. Ellison romanticizes this site by imagining a disembodied womb wherein his protagonist can hibernate only to emerge, some time later, renewed. In chapter 4, "She's a Brick House," about *Corregidora*, I deal with the futility of the gesture as well as some of its gendered implications.

Works Cited

Anzaldúa, Gloria. *Borderlands*/La Frontera: *The New Mestiza*. San Francisco: Spinters-Aunt Lute, 1987.

Faulkner, William. *Go Down, Moses*. New York: Vintage, 1940.

Gudaker, Grey, ed. *Keep Your Head to the Sky: Interpreting African American Home Ground*. Charlottesville: University Press of Virginia, 1999.

Griffin, Farah. *"Who Set You Flowin'?": The African-American Migration Narrative.* New York: Oxford University Press, 1995.

Massey, Doreen. "Double Articulation: A Place in the World." In Angelika Bammer, ed., *Displacements: Cultural Identities in Question.* Bloomington: Indiana University Press, 1994, 110–21.

Ostendorf, Berndt. "Ralph Waldo Ellison: Anthropology, Modernism, and Jazz." In Robert O'Meally, ed., *New Essays on* Invisible Man. New York: Cambridge University Press, 1988, 95–121.

Scarry, Elaine. *The Body in Pain: The Making and the Unmaking of the World.* New York: Oxford University Press, 1985.

Watts, Jerry Gafio. *Heroism and the Black Intellectual: Ralph Ellison, Politics, and Afro-American Intellectual Life.* Chapel Hill: University of North Carolina Press, 1994.

Wright, John S. "The Conscious Hero and the Rites of Man: Ellison's War." In Robert O'Meally, ed., *New Essays on* Invisible Man. New York: Cambridge University Press, 1988, 157–86.

Wright, Richard. *12 Million Black Voices.* New York: Thunder's Mouth Press, 1941.

3

Get in the Kitchen and Rattle Them Pots and Pans: *The Bluest Eye*

Harriet Beecher Stowe and her sister, Catherine Beecher, coauthored a work entitled *The American Woman's Home* for middle-class Victorian women, to help them use the site of home, and specifically the kitchen, as a means of ordering their lives. Home as the domestic sphere, as opposed to the broad geographical landscape of the city, had been deemed, and remains, the woman's realm. Such readings of place are "fundamentally political," to borrow Doreen

Massey's language.[1] In other words, persistent readings of home as the feminine place serve a political end. Yet as Lori Askeland writes, "The vulnerability of this domain, however, must not be overlooked; the house remains a sheltered 'feminine' space, that is, a *hus* for true spiritual growth, which by virtue of its enclosure in the 'masculine' domain of materialism and commercialism, always remains in danger of being invaded and corrupted by it" (782). While the values promoted by Stowe and Beecher's reading of the Victorian "model home" were deconstructed by later writers like Toni Morrison, many of their notions about the site of home persist due to the influence of larger patriarchal paradigms. "The woman's place is in the home"—even if that home abuses, confines, perverts. The home as shelter is an enduring myth that both men and women found reason to support. So even when the built environment did not support the mythology through architectural design, women found ways to imagine a new place. As Askeland explains:

> Implicitly, then, the "model home" represented both shelter from and dominance over the chaos of the world. As several scholars have noted, the kitchen was one place where Stowe and Beecher in particular believed that order and control could be brought to bear on society's problems. . . . [But Victorian homes were not built according to the innovations suggested by these two women.] Thus because their domain was always undermined by their need for shelter in the larger masculine domain, Victorian women were often forced to enact the reverse of Rapoport's dictum: to "think" their domain, create a mental ideal of it, after it had already been built, and thereby remodel as best they could. (787)

Women began "remodeling" within the space of their own imaginations, and the degree to which they were able to act on their thoughts determined the success of their "renovation."

This chapter turns to the material constraints out of which women's experiences are forged. Toni Morrison's representation of home moves away from the concern with the city in Wright's and Ellison's works. Morrison's focal point shifts to the kitchens in *The Bluest Eye*. Thus I shift from the city in the previous chapter that surrounds Bigger's kitchenette apartment and the Daltons' basement in *Native Son* and the ever-changing face of Harlem that contrasts with Mary Rambo's blues kitchen and his well-lit underground hideaway in *Invisible Man*. Presumably, had the narrator of *Invisible Man* been able to go back over the puddles of milk to the home he was running toward during the Harlem riot, he would have found Mary where he left her. While the narrator's identity is so vital that he *cannot* go home again, Mary's presence is so fundamental that she cannot *leave* home. In contrast, in *The Bluest Eye*, Morrison demystifies Mary's blues kitchen by offering first Big Mama's imaginary kitchen, then Mrs. MacTeer's greens and blues kitchen, Polly's black and blue kitchen, and finally the Breedloves' kitchen that seems to have no music, no food, no comfort at all. The dynamic imposed by these kitchen places, so limiting to the vital male protagonists of Wright's and Ellison's novels, is ultimately subverted by the perverse behavior of Cholly Breedlove in his own kitchen.

Central to the construct of home because of its function as hearth that both heats and feeds the household, the kitchen is crucial to the survival of the inhabitants. Even the Thomas family of *Native Son* has an oven, the presence of which justifies the naming of the whole apartment a "kitchenette." Of course, the oven is woefully inadequate in sustaining the family and consequently, the oven/hearth fractures into the consuming furnace in Bigger's alternate place within the Dalton home. Thus the centrality of the kitchen/oven is usurped by the basement/furnace, which, in serving as crematorium for Mary Dalton, holds something even more imperative for Bigger (as well as for Mary's parents) than heat in the middle of a Chicago blizzard.

In Morrison's *Paradise* (1998), the oven is quite literally the center of the town of Haven until the residents feel compelled to move. The town established by former slaves has been threatened by an undefinable "outside":

Ten generations had known what lay Out There: space, once beckoning and free, became unmonitored and seething; became a void where random and organized evil erupted when and where it chose—behind any standing tree, behind the door of any house, humble or grand. . . . But lessons had been learned and relearned in the last three generations about how to protect a town. So, like the ex-slaves who knew what came first, the ex-soldiers broke up the oven and loaded it into two trucks even before they took apart their own beds. (16)

The oven is taken apart brick by brick and moved to the center of the new town, where it is reassembled. The hearth is home for the residents of Haven and later, the newly established Ruby. And, significantly, it is not located inside a kitchen place. Instead it is outside, in the center of the town. Once the oven is removed from the kitchen, just as in *Native Son*, the illusion of (black) female authority is shattered. In *Paradise*, Morrison literally removes the kitchen walls that might otherwise reinforce the pretense of (black) female power, concealing the true male authority that maintains identity, passes along traditions, conducts business, and polices the community.

The material site plays a direct role in authorizing behavior. Moreover, place to some degree can dictate behavior. As both a material and psychological construct, home is given to impose structure and purpose on an otherwise meaningless space. However, if it fails to produce order, then its occupants must create order by some other means. The ultimate tragedy of home as place is that when it fails to be precisely that which it is promoted to be (fixed, inherently locatable, stabilizing), it asserts itself despotically upon the lives of its inhabitants by dictating what they can and cannot do. Yet, rather than being abandoned as a failed, even impossible, construct, it becomes the focus of a power struggle instigated by the politics of place to maintain the elusive/illusionary site of home.

On the most fundamental level, of course, homes are built. Carving physical space into definitive places is an aggressive act. For once space is cut into units of meaning such as room, house, city, state, school, and store, which gain their significance as particular locales in relationship to one another, we who are invested in those distinctions must first acknowledge their existence in these specific terms. Yet it is not enough simply to acknowledge the labels; we must stand ready to defend them. The act of place making, like all other constructions of identity, is necessarily communal. It operates in terms of inclusion and exclusion, and consequently precipitates the construction of binary oppositions like inside versus outside or "us" versus "them"—and these are debatable constructs. Kathleen M. Kirby explains that place operates on the presumption of definitive borders that can be used to determine key aspects of individual identities:

> Place seems to assume set boundaries that one fills to achieve a solid identity. Place settles space into objects, working to reinscribe the Cartesian monad and the autonomous ego. It perpetuates the fixed perimeters of ontological categories, making them coherent containers of essences, in relation to which one must be "inside" or "out," native" or "foreign," in the same way that one can, in the Euclidean universe, at least, be in only one place at one time. (176)

Once these boundaries demarcating the perimeters of place have been established, place begins to dictate which human activities should occur there and elsewhere, and moreover, is endowed with the ability to construct signposts of identities in order to determine who should participate in which activities. The inhabitants necessarily enter into a struggle. Henri Lefebvre explains that space is not simply a void waiting to be filled by a fertile presence; instead, it functions as a mechanism of power: "That space signifies is incontestable. But what it signifies is dos and don'ts—and this brings us back to power. Power's message is invariably confused—deliberately so; dissemination is necessarily part of any message from power" (142).[2] Place is conflicted, and the intensity of the struggle surrounding spatial delineations is dictated by the level of commitment and power occupants have to apply to defending them. Thus, for example, in Morrison's *The Bluest Eye*, Pecola Breedlove is the most completely victimized because she is the weakest person in the struggle.

The tragedy of place is demonstrated with dramatic clarity by Pecola's rape at the hands of her father. Preceding this devastating climax, however, are indications that more than simply address *how* these events come to pass, as the narrator, Claudia, modestly asserts in the early pages of the novel, but *why* as well. For Pecola, home never succumbs to the order of place because place has no structure in the Breedlove home, which therefore does not function as place. Instead the claim of groundedness, articulated by "home as place," that circumscribes knowledge of and experiences with home, is contradicted by the lack of order. And the disorder that might otherwise be accepted as space or unencoded expanse is contradicted by the material structure built as house (home). This home, then, is left dysfunctional. Without structure, Pecola finds only the chaos that leads to her dementia within the amorphous abyss of blue eyes. While she experiences the complete loss of meaning and value for her own subject position, some of those around her are able to maintain a semblance of order in their lives. Sites of meaning often appear for other (female) characters in the oasis offered by the blues kitchen, like the one Mary Rambo has in *Invisible Man*, that serves to translate the pain of experiences and deprivation of present conditions into the cathartic form of blues expressiveness.

Our examination of home for the male characters Bigger and the narrator of *Invisible Man* goes outside of the structure to grapple with the geographically larger sites of the city and thus alludes to the imagery of state and nation. Bigger encounters the city and kills two women who threaten his survival there, and the invisible man must leave women behind. In contrast, our study of home for the female character, Pecola, leads further inside, to a room within the structure (to grapple with the physically smaller site of the kitchen that evokes the imagery of family and nourishment). It is no mere coincidence that for the narrator in *Invisible Man*, Mary is figured as a mother *in* her kitchen—located safely under patriarchal control. Despite the potentiality signified by Mary Rambo's blues kitchen, the male protagonist there has more options available when he begins engineering the site of home than does a little girl like Pecola. Home for her centers around her family, and her mother in particular.

Kitchen: Mrs. MacTeer's Greens and Blues Kitchen

The closest Morrison comes to Mary Rambo's blues kitchen in *Invisible Man* is Mrs. MacTeer's kitchen. Mustard greens are cooking there instead of cabbage. Greens, like cabbage, are African American soul food. As in *Native Son*, when Bigger's hunger helps him forget he is not at home (sopping his plate clean with bread),[3] and in *Invisible Man,* when the narrator enjoys the hot, buttery yams that remind him of his cultural heritage in the South, the greens play a key role in making Mrs. MacTeer's home. Morrison uses the word "greens" as a pun, introducing a play that deliberately conflates the taste and the smell of the greens with the sound of the singing and the experience of place.

While Mrs. MacTeer is not singing in her kitchen when we meet her, even as a young child, Claudia MacTeer notices the effect her mother's kitchen blues have on the mood of the house. Lonesome Saturdays are transformed by song:

If my mother was in a singing mood, it wasn't so bad. She would sing about hard times, bad times, and somebody-done-gone-and-left-me times. But her voice was so sweet and her singing-eyes so melty I found myself longing for these hard times, yearning to be grown without "a thin di-i-ime to my name." I looked forward to the delicious time when "my man" would leave me, when I would "hate to see that evening sun go down . . ." 'cause then I would know "my man has left this town." Misery colored by the greens and blues in my mother's voice took all the grief out of the words, and left me with a conviction that pain was not only endurable, it was sweet.

But without song, those Saturdays sat on my head like a coal scuttle, and if Mama was fussing, as she was now, it was like somebody throwing stones at it. (24)

The blues, of course, thrive within a culture of contestation. Mrs. MacTeer is fluent enough in a blues vernacular to rid many "lonesome Saturdays" of their bitterness, but Claudia states clearly that there are moments when her mother's blues idiom fails. One such occasion is in autumn, soon after the novel opens, when Pecola Breedlove comes to stay with the MacTeer family.

Mrs. MacTeer makes no secret of the fact that Pecola will not be staying long since she is irritated with the girl at the moment. The curt manner with which Mrs. MacTeer deals with Pecola mirrors her expressions of love to her own daughters, Frieda and Claudia. Her concern for Pecola's well-being is tempered by her poverty. Once she discovers that the visitor has drunk three quarts of milk over the course of a single day, she begins a harangue implicating Pecola and everyone else by whom she feels she has been wronged. The milk becomes a symbol that incriminates Pecola's family and her mother, in particular, for their failure to nurture or even properly nourish her. Pecola can drink three quarts of milk, but she remains thirsty for the love that Mrs. Breedlove refuses to give her.

Mrs. MacTeer assumes Pecola's motivation for drinking the milk is greed, but Claudia understands it to have another source—her desire to engage the picture of Shirley Temple on the cup. Both Frieda and Pecola talk of how they adore her. Pecola imbibes the milk because it gives her the opportunity to worship the image of Shirley Temple; it is a simple conduit legitimating her relationship with the girl on the cup. She drinks the milk like an insatiable infant who believes that by drinking she will somehow become closer to that cute and adored image. What she discovers, unfortunately, is that her efforts only cause her further alienation.

Pecola is thrown away by her family and left to sink or swim at the mercy of God or the world around her. Neither of her parents bothers to check on her well-being. Unlike Shirley Temple, who seems to have nearly the whole world's love, Pecola has few who care whether she lives or dies, and they are not empowered to do much to alleviate her suffering. Pecola's presence is like the presence of the cup in the MacTeer home. The cup suggests a value system decreeing who is or who is not lovable in society. The image that gives complex meaning to an otherwise insignificant cup, bolster the mainstream's claim of ownership over the ideal American home. Even if icons such as Shirley Temple serve to anger or dismiss, as for Claudia and Pecola respectively, they have managed to infiltrate the MacTeer household, creating confusion and keeping it a site of contestation.

While Mrs. MacTeer overlooks the negative significance of both the cup and blue-eyed dolls, Claudia is acutely aware of their devastating potential. Instead of offering a character like Mary Rambo, who consistently expresses herself in a blues idiom, Morrison juxtaposes Mrs. MacTeer's moments of failed blues expressiveness with Claudia's naïve insight. Claudia destroys the doll she is given for Christmas in an effort to expose its value. In scenes like the following, Claudia's latent blues expressiveness incubates, only to erupt in gestures such as the dismantling of the doll:

> I fingered the face, wondering at the single-stroke eyebrows; picked at the pearly teeth stuck like piano keys between red bowline lips. Traced the turned-up nose, poked the glassy blue eyeballs, twisted yellow hair. I could not love it. But I could examine it to see what it was that all the world said was lovable. (20)

Claudia speaks as the uncorrupted voice of a threatened black subjectivity. As Gurleen Grewal asserts, "Morrison's invocation of black music is significant, for it related to a nonbourgeois consciousness not co-opted by the dominant culture" (16). Rather than literal music, the black "music" here is the sentiment of the blues. Claudia employs this blues logic even as a child. She is as perplexed by the adults' response to the doll as they are by hers. Her mother assumes that she desires the unyielding plastic white doll for Christmas; no one asks her what she wants. If they had, she would have been ready with an answer:

> "I want to sit on the low stool in Big Mama's kitchen with my lap full of lilacs and listen to Big Papa play his violin for me alone." The lowness of the stool made for my body, the security and warmth of Big Mama's kitchen, the smell of the lilacs, the sound of the music. . . . (21)

Importantly, what Claudia wants for Christmas is to experience a kitchen scene wherein she is central. The scale of an adult area is

brought into proportion by her "low stool." The kitchen is both secure and warm due to her relationship with and proximity to her
grandparents. This experience is characteristically vernacular and
resists the force imposed by the dominant structure as represented
by the Shirley Temple cup and the doll.

It's no wonder that the adults do not ask Claudia what she wants
for Christmas, since they could not have given her what she desires.
Barbara Johnson's observations made in reference to *Sula* are ap-
plicable here:

> Morrsion's novel conveys so strong a sense of what she calls "rootedness"
> precisely by writing under the sign of uprootedness. Yet it is not simply
> that there was once a *there* there and now it is gone, but that there is
> from the beginning something profoundly uncanny about "that place."
> Home is familiar precisely to the extent that, as Renita Weems puts it, it
> is somehow a place one has never been. (4)

Claudia has never been figured in Big Mama's kitchen in the ways
she imagines. The "experience" there is the sole item on Claudia's
Christmas wish list. Claudia imagines the interior space of Big
Mama's kitchen to be without contradictions. There are no appara-
tuses like the cup and the doll to disrupt the fantasy in which she
is central. However, we know that "real" space is fraught with contradictions. Building upon Steve Pile's work in *The Body and the
City: Psychoanalysis, Space, and Subjectivity*, Katherine McKittrick
asserts that multiple narratives simultaneously compete for space:

> Homes and the nation become hybrid intercultural spaces that encour-
> age different kinds of ambivalence in the mind. . . . Pile explains that
> spaces—emotional, bodily and environmental—produce "many spaces
> in the same space: space projected from the inside onto the surface of
> the body. . . . Objects forever preserved within the body-mind; outsides
> inside; insides outside. . . . Lines of demarcation, ideals; and so on. . . ."
> There is a messiness, then, to occupying space, and in *The Bluest Eye* the
> relationship between place and identity is about mental and corporeal
> movement, is cursive inscriptions, naturalisation, and contestation. The
> inside is out, and vice versa. (13)

As is evidenced by the environment outside of Claudia's imagination, identity for a black girl in 1941 Lorain, Ohio is contested.

But for Claudia, contradictions are mediated by eruptions of blues expressiveness. As Grewal explains, "What makes it possible for . . . [Claudia] to resist the dominant culture is the strong presence of an alternative culture at home passed on to her by her mother, whose blues songs . . . and kitchen conversation with the neighborhood black women . . . emit the resilience of a cultural identity of resistance" (37). Pecola, on the other hand, cannot even imagine an experience like that of which Claudia dreams. The intimacy of Big Mama's kitchen site is the polar extreme of the detachment fostered by the "outdoors." So while one girl has a fantasy in which she is solidly placed (at home), the other girl is operating out of another fantasy in which she is maximally displaced (homeless).

Pecola comes to be in the MacTeer home as a "case" who needs a place to live for a few days because she and her family are "outdoors." Claudia explains what that means: "There is a difference between being put out and being put outdoors. If you are put *out*, you go somewhere else; if you are out*doors*, there is no place to go. The distinction was subtle but final. Outdoors was the end of something, an irrevocable, physical fact; defining and complementing our metaphysical condition" (18). Being outdoors suggests a literal homelessness that means more to the community than the abstractions of race and class because of its tangibility. Nothing elicited more sympathy or fear in Lorain, Ohio than the thought of being put outdoors. The experience is no more "real" than the scene Claudia imagines of Big Mama's kitchen because, likewise, it is a place imagined without contradictions. The community agrees to overlook discrepancies that might suggest that "outdoors" is anything other than what it needs that space to be.

Claudia informs the readers that Pecola is "outdoors," then explains what it means in order to dissipate any confusion that might arise from the fact that Pecola actually first appears inside. In fact, Claudia and Frieda have graciously agreed to set aside petty arguments so that they can focus their attention on "trying hard to keep her from feeling outdoors" (19). The reality is, of course, that the Breedloves are not literally outside. Each of them has some-place to stay until they can be reunited. Pecola's father, Cholly, is in jail for setting their residence on fire; her brother is with another family; and Mrs. Breedlove is staying with the Fishers, where she works as a maid. They are not forced to lounge in the gutters like those mired in the contemporary, urban sense of homelessness. Yet the exercise of these two little girls is futile within a community that needs to have the Breedloves "outdoors." A more mature Claudia later admits:

> All of us—all who knew her—felt so wholesome after we cleaned our-selves on her. We were so beautiful when we stood astride her ugliness. Her simplicity decorated us, her guilt sanctified us, her pain made us glow with health, her awkwardness made us believe we were eloquent. Her poverty kept us generous. Even her waking dreams we used—to silence our own nightmares. And she let us, and thereby deserved our contempt. We honed our egos on her, padded our characters with her frailty; and yawned in the fantasy of our strength. (159)

The community balances its own insecurities against Pecola as if their positive characteristics could only exist when directly con-fronted by the opposite extreme. She embodies the negative traits those around her never wanted to be—black, ugly, poor, etc.—and they use her as a scapegoat to free themselves of being identified as those things. So even as Pecola has a place to rest her head in the MacTeer home, she is still "outdoors" because she cannot—is not allowed to—stay in the place where she is. Marc C. Conner ob-serves that "the house serves as the antidote to the evil of being out-doors, offering shelter and safety. . . . But the home as the haven is soon translated into the home as prison. . . . The house is simulta-neously respite and jail; like the community, for which it stands as synecdoche, the house seems to promise rest and comfort, but it provides neither, especially for Pecola" (53). While the house con-figured simultaneously as respite and prison might be more clearly illustrated by a text like Harriet Jacobs's *Incidents in the Life of a Slave Girl*, the dynamic, as Conner suggests, is played out here also.

Jacobs's protagonist, Linda Brent, experiences both rest and imprisonment as a fugitive in the confines of her grandmother's home; here, Morrison creates a triumvirate.[4] The polar, imaginary experiences of Claudia in Big Mama's kitchen (at home) and Pecola's experience of being "outdoors" (homeless) diverge from the more "real" and, at least within this context, more central locale marked by Mrs. MacTeer's kitchen.

Kitchen: Polly's Black and Blue Kitchen

Mrs. Breedlove escapes the fate of homelessness after Cholly puts their family outdoors because she can stay at the Fishers' home. Polly's kitchen is a "black" place in the ways that Dilsey's kitchen is in *The Sound and the Fury*—a place where Pauline Breedlove serves her surrogate white daughter and her white family. Mrs. Breedlove is resentful of intrusions into this realm, which might remind her of the ugliness of her life at the storefront. While she is leery of defending that place, she is fierce in defense of Fisher family affairs. In this other place, her employers' kitchen, Mrs. Breedlove seems to escape the repercussions associated with her own family. Here she can lord over canned goods, shiny floors, and other things that seem to give her life value: "Power, praise, and luxury were hers in this household. They even gave her what she had never had—a nickname—Polly" (101).

Even the little pink-and-yellow girl at the Fishers' home calls Mrs. Breedlove "Polly." Hearing the name from the lips of a child younger than she incites Claudia to anger: "Her calling Mrs. Breedlove Polly, when even Pecola called her mother Mrs. Breedlove, seemed reason enough to scratch her" (86). The designation, which seems arrogant and disrespectful to Claudia, contributes to Mrs. Breedlove's possessiveness over the space of this home. She is able to function within a relatively viable construction of "ideal servant," which, although constrictive, is nonetheless a seductive contrast to the ugliness of her life at home. Rather than deconstructing such designations, as Claudia does in her dismemberment of the doll or as Bigger Thomas does by decapitating the murdered corpse of Mary Dalton in *Native Son*, Mrs. Breedlove accepts her role within the Shirley Temple world signified by the cup. So while Pecola hungrily laps at the white milk to no avail, as mammy, her mother is received into this alternative household. Claudia describes the effect the kitchen has on Mrs. Breedlove: "Mrs. Breedlove's skin glowed like taffeta in the reflection of white porcelain, white woodwork, polished cabinets, and brilliant copperware" (86)—and it is Polly, of course, who keeps the kitchen glowing. Her presence in the pink-and-yellow girl's kitchen is as vital to maintaining the whiteness of the cabinetry, the counters, and the family who lives there as the black drops are in the optic white paint of *Invisible Man*'s Liberty Paint Factory.

Conversely, Pecola is the one black drop too many. Pecola's presence in the Fisher household disrupts the precarious balance and threatens to destroy the whole system. She is only there to handle a chore for her mother, and she is not even invited in until Claudia and Frieda arrive. With a stern admonition to stay still, Mrs. Breedlove leaves the three girls in the kitchen. When she returns with a bag of wet laundry and to answer the small child's call, Mrs. Breedlove discovers that Pecola has accidentally knocked over a freshly baked pie and is hopping around the floor in its hot insides: "In one gallop she was on Pecola, and with the back of her hand knocked her on the floor. Pecola slid in the pie juice, one leg folding under her. Mrs. Breedlove yanked her up by the arm, slapped her again, and in a voice thin with anger, abused Pecola directly and Frieda and me by implication" (86).

Polly's maternal feelings seem to be directed at the pink-and-yellow child rather than her own daughter's obvious humiliation and pain. It is the black child who is hurt and sliding across the floor in the dark juice, yet Mrs. Breedlove is invested in whiteness and defends her place in it without realizing that she has internalized the terms of her own oppression. Just as the narrator of *Invisible Man* must be expelled from the Liberty Paint Factory, so too must Pecola be expelled from the Fisher household. This kitchen, like the other kitchen site in the storefront, serves as a place of torment for Pecola. So the dimension of physical violence is added to her experience of this material "black" site. Instead of a blues kitchen like the one that mediates on behalf of Claudia, with greens flavoring the sound of her mother's singing, the "black" place of Polly's kitchen, a place of domestic servitude, becomes for Pecola a "black and blue" place.

Because of its proximity to the white household, Polly's kitchen is a "black" site, and unlike the characters seen in their "own" kitchens, Polly does not have a blues vocabulary with which to temper the despotism of that site. Unlike Bigger Thomas, who is frustrated by his "relief" job at the Dalton home, Polly laps up her job as domestic for the Fisher family as readily as Pecola drinks the three quarts of milk. The household that keeps Pauline from being outside when her husband, Cholly, sets their house on fire cannot accommodate her children. This house, then, serves as both Pauline's refuge and her prison in the way that Conner suggests. To stay there, she must reject her family, and in so doing she sacrifices crucial parts of herself. Barbara Johnson notes in her psychoanalytical reading of *Sula* that "Freud exclaims over the fact that the German word for 'homey' extends itself to turn into its opposite—that the meaning of 'heimlich' moves with a kind of inevitability from cozy, comfortable, and familiar to hidden, secret, and strange, so that one meaning of 'heimlich' is identitcal to its opposite, 'unheimlich'" (4). In the German sense of the word, home is at once home and not home. Consequently, Pauline is fragmented into multiple selves who mirror Morrison's earlier triumvirate: Mrs. Breedlove's experiences at the storefront (homelessness) and Polly's at the Fishers' (at home) are mediated by Pauline's memories of her teenaged years.

Long before Pauline became Polly or even Mrs. Breedlove, she had stepped on a rusty nail and was left with a mild deformity in one of her feet:

> Slight as it was this deformity explained for her many things that would have been otherwise incomprehensible: why she alone of all the children had no nickname; why there were no funny jokes and anecdotes about funny things she had done; why no one ever remarked on her food preferences. . . . Why she never felt at home anywhere, or that she belonged

anyplace. Her general feeling of separateness and unworthiness she blamed on her foot. Restricted, as a child, to this cocoon of her family's spinning, she cultivated quiet and private pleasures. She liked, most of all, to arrange things. To line things up in rows—jars on shelves at canning, peach pits on the step, sticks, stones, leaves—and the members of her family let these arrangements be. (88)

The significance of common occurrences such as teasing and nick-naming is easily overlooked. These communal practices bind individuals around a shared past and give them a sense of cohesiveness that helps unite them into a family unit.[5] Being excluded from these practices leaves Pauline feeling isolated. She acknowledges her sense of alienation and identifies her misshapen foot as the source of her world's failings. Her foot is the foundation upon which she builds a vocabulary for interpreting an "incomprehensible" situation. Without this key element, the young Pauline has no means of systematically confronting the chaos of her life. Her family has excluded her from the cultural practices that structure their existence and left her alone to develop a framework for rendering her experiences intelligible.

For brief periods during her early adulthood, Pauline does experience moments of blues expressiveness. Cholly comes with music—"a kind of city-street music where laughter belies anxiety, and joy is as short and straight as the blade of a pocket knife. She listened carefully to the music and let it pull her lips into a smile" (91). So when she narrates her experience of meeting him for the first time, she expresses herself in a rare blues idiom: "When I first seed Cholly, I want you to know it was like all the bits of color from that time down home when all us chil'ren went berry picking after a funeral and I put some in the pocket of my Sunday dress, and they masked up and stained my hips. My whole dress was messed with purple, and it never did wash out. Not the dress nor me" (91–92). Cat Moses suggests that Pauline articulates a blues narrative of her own, "in lyrically expressing a longing for the rural Southern community that revolved around church ("Sunday dress") and ritual ("berry picking," "funeral"), Pauline accomplishes what the blues singer accomplishes: she recreates that which is lost and for which she longs, transforming lack into poetry. Unfortunately, the transformation is temporary and exists only in her memory" (6). Pauline divests herself of the value of such expressive gestures that paint her experiences with color in favor of more calculated, less intuitive systems. The exclusion she feels manifests itself as restriction, so she founds her teleology on "quiet and private pleasures" rather than social practices like those of her family:

> She liked, most of all, to arrange things. To line things up in rooms—jars on shelves at canning, peach pits on the step, sticks, stones, leaves—and the members of her family let these arrangements be. . . . During all of her four years of going to school, she was enchanted by numbers and depressed by words. She missed—without knowing what she missed— paints and crayons. (88–89)

This teleology operates like blues expressiveness to fulfill the psychological need for order in Pauline's life. However, the smallness of her spatial terrain dictates the smallness of the system she employs. She is relegated to the porch step and the kitchen, left alone to give order to trivialities that neither impose upon nor impede the welfare of others.

While the omnipresence and deprivation of her foot motivate Pauline to find a way to maintain her mental faculties, they also serve, later in life, to draw her effectively into complicity with her own victimization and, subsequently, that of her daughter. The space of the Fishers' kitchen (the site where she becomes "ideal servant") and the porch step are so constricted that the system Pauline has erected to order her life is not able to accommodate anyone other than herself. Because it does not interfere, her childhood family allows her the privilege of that order, but later as a mother she is not able to derive creative expressiveness from the system that might protect her children also. So just as if someone had doomed her to act out a tragic script written at the time her foot was permanently marked by that nail, Mrs. Breedlove refuses to read any signs as warnings and instead accepts them almost fondly, as fate.[6] This is how she comes to have ugly children and to live in an abusive home.

The children Sammy and Pecola are ugly because she and Cholly are ugly. Their ugliness is a simple confirmation of what her foot, missing front tooth, and newfound education at the movies[7] had already told her—that she and her family are not worthy of either attention or love. As the rotten seed planted by this derision festers, Mrs. Breedlove comes to despise those things and people who are most closely allied with her: "More and more she neglected her house, her children, her man—they were like the afterthoughts one has just before sleep, the early-morning and late evening edges of her day, the dark edges that made the daily life with the Fishers lighter, more delicate, more lovely" (101). In the Fisher home, Mrs. Breedlove finds affirmation that she does not get elsewhere: "Really, she is the ideal servant" (101). She hungrily accepts her position as maid because it offers her a place to escape the ugliness she believes characterizes the rest of her life.

Kitchen: The Breedloves' Kitchen

The Breedloves' storefront has very few interior walls. The kitchen is a separate room, but the bedroom and living area are distinguished primarily by furnishings. In this regard, the storefront is similar to the kitchenette apartments of Chicago and the Truebloods' cabin in *Invisible Man*. For reasons discussed in the previous chapters, such living conditions affect people's lives in sometimes rather disturbing ways. As Richard Wright laments in *12 Million Black Voices*, "The kitchenette blights the personalities of our growing children, disorganizes them, blinds them to hope, creates problems whose effects can be traced in the characters of its child victims for years afterward. . . . The kitchenette fills our black boys with longing and restlessness, urging them to run off from home" (110–11). The same effects are evident in the lives of Pecola and Sammy Breedlove. "[Sammy] was known, by the time he was fourteen, to have run away from home no less than twenty-seven times. . . . Pecola, on the other hand, restricted by youth and sex, experimented with methods of endurance. Though the methods varied, the pain was as consistent as it was deep" (38). The storefront is not a hospitable place to live. As Shelley Wong asserts, "Nowhere in this novel is this legacy of slavery—the disfigurement of human relationships by the marketplace—more ironically stated than in Morrison's decision to locate a family by the name of 'Breedlove' in a converted (and poorly converted at that) storefront" (462).

Drinking, having sex, fighting, sleeping, and even waking up are all spectacles available for "public" display, in the Breedlove home. It seems that nothing can happen in this storefront without everyone present at the time knowing about it. The physical barriers that would serve as signposts, issuing prohibitions ("Do not enter"; "Do not exit"; "Watch this, not that") are simply not present. In their place is space with very few socializing directives. Thus few barriers exist to separate girlhood experiences, like Claudia's Christmas wish, from adult episodes, like the times when Mrs. Breedlove will not allow herself to have an orgasm until she knows that "my flesh is all that be on . . . [Cholly's] mind" (103). Her parents do not shelter Pecola. Instead, she is forced to confront situations that they might have veiled for her. Furthermore, she has never had access to childhood experiences like the one that Claudia imagines in Big Mama's kitchen, that function as signs of love, so she is left to interpret her parents' sexual intercourse through her own limited knowledge:

> Into her eyes came the picture of Cholly and Mrs. Breedlove in bed. He making sounds as though he were in pain, as though something had him by the throat and wouldn't let go. Terrible as his noises were, they were not nearly as bad as no noise at all from her mother. It was as though she was not even there. Maybe that was love. Choking sounds and silence. (48–49)

Because Pecola is forced to confront her parents' sexuality, she imagines that this is love.[8] Certainly, walls create an illusion of safety that can, and indeed must, be challenged. But walls also serve to foster the sense of security a young girl needs until such time as she develops into a mature adult.

The fact that the walls are around the kitchen and not a bedroom, for example, is a measure of Mrs. Breedlove's inadequacy. In this statement I do not mean to absolve Cholly of his charge within the household; however, we must carefully examine the power at work here. While Mrs. Breedlove cannot be held responsible as an architect, literally designing walls, it is she, in particular, who superintends many of the spatial dynamics. The walls around the kitchen serve as a normalizing gesture that helps to distinguish the storefront as a home. Mrs. Breedlove is able to identify with this particular site and the norms the kitchen seeks to represent (that of the hearth). By acting out the role of wife and mother in her gestures of caretaking, she demonstrates her investment in maintaining the illusion of normality. "Mrs. Breedlove considered herself an upright and Christian woman, burdened with a no-count man, whom God wanted her to punish" (37). The kitchen, then, becomes a mere tool she uses, along with its accoutrements, to maintain her perceived authority.

On a Saturday morning near the beginning of the novel, these dynamics are played out in a ceremonial conclusion to one of Cholly's drunken episodes. Mrs. Breedlove's actions, as the narrator recounts, are well choreographed: "in the kitchen . . . [Mrs. Breedlove] made noises with doors, faucets, and pans. The noises were hollow, but the threats they implied were not. . . . There was direction and purpose in Mrs. Breedlove's movements that had nothing to do with the preparation of breakfast" (35). The eruptions of violence in the Breedlove household can be gauged on Saturday mornings like this one by the clamor in the kitchen. These sounds function similarly to those Mrs. MacTeer makes in her (blues) kitchen to influence her daughter's perceptions and to shape the order and events of the day. But the regularity with which these menacing sounds emanate from this kitchen is not balanced by the comfort offered by the smell of mustard greens cooking on the stove and songs, "about hard times, bad times, and somebody-done-gone-and-left-me times" (24) that make life tolerable for Claudia and her mother in the MacTeer house. Mrs. Breedlove uses frying pans and pokers as weapons rather than for cooking and tending the stove.

This kitchen serves Mrs. Breedlove's needs as much as the Fisher kitchen does. Her role in relationship to the family, however, is inverted. Where she embraces the Fisher family, she rejects her own. Here again we are reminded of Barbara Johnson's use of Freud's notion of *heimlich*; clearly, Mrs. Breedlove's storefront home is also, simultaneously, not home. The Breedloves' kitchen is not a place of soul food and singing, like the kitchen in the MacTeer household and Mary Rambo's blues kitchen from *Invisible Man*. Instead, Mrs. Breedlove's kitchen is the ceremonial backdrop for repercussions of routine episodes of drunkenness.

Womb: Collapsing Inward

If *The Bluest Eye* is a study of spatial politics, then the struggle comes down to a battle between Cholly and Pecola: he is a sign of boundless passion and operates without restraint; she is passion without an outlet. The former bursts outward and the latter collapses inward. Energy seeks the most expedient route to the ground; thus given their proximity, Cholly finds Pecola the most expedient conduit for his expression. She has no order or meaning apart from the perception of her ugliness to use as a framework for interpretation, so space collapses inward.

The Breedloves' kitchen is dysfunctional because they have placed no restrictions on the activities authorized to happen there. Each character attempts to flee the stultifying power of the constructs imposed by this storefront home in his or her own way. Mrs. Breedlove rejects all but the most superficial connections to her family for her identity as Polly in the Fisher home. Sammy runs away for however long he can manage. Cholly drinks as an escape. Pecola has the least effective means of escape, with her earnest desire to become beautiful by turning her eyes blue.[9]

So the perception of ever-extending, empty expanse, which has already been condensed for Pecola by the impermeability of the kitchen walls, is further condensed by the lack of interpersonal directives that might order or restrict any activity. Consequently, all that remains to define the perimeters of the kitchen are the unpredictable impulses of Cholly Breedlove. Cholly invades Pecola's body as territory and establishes borders, thereby constructing an extended realm for his expression of pleasure and domination. The deprivation created by this unstructured chaos leads to Pecola's dementia.

Perhaps more than any other character depicted in the novel, Pecola lives the contradictions expressed by the blues. Yet she has no understanding of blues culture or its significance. The "hollow" sounds Mrs. Breedlove makes in the kitchen do not contain the substance of the blues that makes grief seem "sweet." In fact, at the one moment in the novel when Pecola articulates a blues refrain, she is *outside* of her home and lying in bed with the other girls at the MacTeer home. Earlier the neighbor child, Rosemary, presumed when she saw Pecola with her panties down that the girls were "playing nasty." Actually, they had been assisting Pecola because she had just "become a woman." The shared feelings of confusion, fear, frustration, and finally revelation among female characters after this encounter dealing with Pecola's first menstrual cycle lead the young girls to try to express themselves through the language of the blues.

The pain of experience itself, not deliberate effort, compels Pecola to inquire about her new procreative abilities using the syntax of the blues. After Frieda explains that before you can make a baby "somebody has to love you," Pecola asks, "'How do you do that? I mean, how do you get somebody to love you?' But Frieda was asleep. And [Claudia] didn't know" (29). Unfortunately, Pecola does not sustain the potentially transcendent expressiveness of this moment; she locates the failure of her home and family to nurture her in sight rather than in sound—the blues of her eyes rather than the blues of her mouth.

Characters like Mrs. MacTeer and Claudia use blues expressiveness to temper the harsh experiences of their lives. The blues serves to codify place with signposts that offer Claudia direction as she navigates her surroundings. So Claudia first appears with her sister, Frieda, in a naïve blues moment, trying to utter the "right words" over seeds they plant in the ground. Of the few in the community who care enough to pay Pecola attention, it is only the young girls, Claudia and Frieda, who think her baby is worth saving: "So deeply concerned were we with the health and safe delivery of Pecola's baby we could think of nothing but our own magic: if we planted the seeds, and said the right words over them, they would blossom, and everything would be all right" (9). However, as Michael Awkward argues, language fails in *The Bluest Eye* to express the "right words":

> For in the face of Pecola's intense self-hatred and the disdain of an entire community where Pecola and her pregnancy are concerned, discursive acts such as the MacTeer girls' incantations of putative (but, curiously unspoken in the novel) "right words" cannot avoid being anything but insufficient. What is required . . . is the bonding of women, or what Ntozake Shange calls in *For Colored Girls'* final scene of an achieved female community which, not coincidentally, is directly preceded by a male's murder of children—"a laying on of [female] hands." This communal laying on of hands results in the liberation of the female self and "the holiness of myself released." (119)

Pecola does not have access to this communal female healing. Her mother does not bring the milk that she desires and the milk she drinks from the Shirley Temple cup cannot satiate her thirst; instead, it results in a backlash from Mrs. MacTeer about why she cannot satisfy Pecola either. Rather than a female laying on of hands that might offer spiritual renewal and healing, home leaves Pecola bereft of maternal sensitivities and alone to deal with perverse fatherhood: Cholly's destructive masculine laying on of hands. The earth itself refuses to yield for Pecola, and there are no "right words" to say over a child impregnated by her father that will make it otherwise.

Both the words and the ground are crucial here. Even as children, these girls know that they might speak something that can be vital to their ability to negotiate the dynamics of place. Ultimately, the earth proves to be more powerful than their "right words," which cannot intercede to save Pecola or her child. But in choosing to tell Pecola's story, an older Claudia gains authority that the younger Claudia has yet to acquire. *The Bluest Eye* becomes, as Cat Moses describes it in "The Blues Aesthetic in Toni Morrison's *The Bluest Eye*," Claudia's blues narrative.

On the other hand, to survive the kind of assaults directed at her, Pecola needs to reinterpret painful experiences in order to render them intelligible. But the conflict she confronts is too powerful for her meager defense—the hope of becoming pretty. In a dysfunctional household without order, it is even more important that Pecola have a viable means of offense, or at least of coping. Without either, however, Pecola is unable to lessen the tragic impact of the inevitable confrontation. Place is even more constricted for her than the sites of the porch and the Fishers' kitchen are for her mother. Without codifiers to organize her surroundings around a set of established norms, like the walls of a more traditional house[10] or the blues idiom of the MacTeer household,[11] the Breedloves' kitchen randomly signifies contradictory, odd, and even perverse demands that function as expressions of power. If barriers are not established to maintain the order that might protect and defend inhabitants, then the power naturally levels any restrictions. Rather like electricity, power seeks the conductor offering the least resistance as it makes its way to the ground. Pecola is that medium.

Pecola's story is, of course, framed by the narrative of the Dick and Jane primer and its depiction of the green-and-white house. Yet as Wong suggests, its message conceals a problematic interrelationship between residents and the places they occupy:

> The lesson of this passage in fact goes well beyond acknowledging or presenting white bourgeois values—it goes as far as enacting the very conditions of alienated self-containment which underlie those values. We might note, for instance, that the "house" precedes the "family" in order of both appearance and discussion. In this scheme of things, human relations are preempted by property and commodity relations. (472)

Just as Mr. Norton notices the log cabins before he sees the women in *Invisible Man,* the built structure appears first. The primer hearkens back to the Victorian "model home" that Stowe and Beecher extol in *The American Woman's Home*; however, in both Morrison's obvious manipulation of conventions and this more subtle dynamic highlighted by Wong, the primer reveals the essential need for imaginative "remodeling." Without such renovations, place remains despotic.

Pecola's rape attests to the devastating potential of ideological constructs permitted to cohabit freely in the Breedlove storefront. As Wayne Franklin and Michael Steiner explain, "We experience issues such as consumerism, colonialism and patriarchy in concrete locales, whether those locales be the high-toned architecture of a department store, the partitions imposed on a countryside by a foreign power, or the domestic sphere as a material—not just ideological construct. It is the rare human issue that is truly placeless" (4). As a site of culture, this storefront—which is neither house nor home in any mythical sense—implicates larger issues of consumerism, colonialism, and patriarchy, among others. Morrison suggests that incest is *placed* in this storefront at the perverse intersection of racism, poverty, the failure of community, and unfulfilled desire.

That fateful Saturday afternoon when Cholly staggers in drunk, he sees his daughter in the kitchen, washing dishes. Pecola is fulfilling the role she has inherited from her mother. And Cholly barely distinguishes between mother and daughter. She reminds him of Pauline when he met her in Kentucky. "[Pecola's] hands were going around and around a frying pan, scraping flecks of black into cold, greasy dishwater. The timid, tucked-in look of the scratching toe—that was what Pauline was doing the first time he saw her in Kentucky. Leaning over a fence staring at nothing in particular" (128). Pecola makes a similar gesture to the one her mother made years earlier, her foot scratching a place on the back of her leg. Cholly wants to scratch the itch with his teeth. "The confused mixture of memories of Pauline and the doing of a wild and forbidden thing excited him, and a bolt of desire ran down his genitals, giving it length" (128). As always, Cholly acts upon his impulse.

Cholly is contrasted with Mr. MacTeer, who defends his daughter, Frieda, from the illicit, predatory advances of Mr. Henry. Cholly becomes the predator. He does not gauge his actions against a scale of right or wrong, so it never occurs to him that he should not touch his daughter like this: "The creamy toe of her bare foot scratching a velvet leg. It was such a small and simple gesture, but it filled him then with a wondering softness. Not the usual lust to part tight legs with his own, but a tenderness, a protectiveness. A desire to cover her foot with his hand and gently nibble away the itch from the calf with his teeth" (128). He rapes Pecola on the floor in front of the sink. The tragedy of home for Pecola is described best in this scene. The space of home has become so compressed that she is left to maneuver psychologically within the confined space of the kitchen floor.

In 1941 the unyielding black ground signified the terrible cost at which home might be established for the black community of Lorain, Ohio. The barriers that delineate the place of home are erected upon this foundation: the unyielding black ground and the Breedloves' kitchen floor. The storefront is what remains for cultural outcasts like the Breedlove family. Their internalization of white normative values and their inability to find any productive coping mechanisms ultimately pin Pecola tragically to the ground under the weight of her father's "embrace."

Her escape into madness only leaves her more completely bound. The expanse of space that had been segmented into home/kitchen is further condensed into the stultifying and incestuous site of Pecola's own body, raped and impregnated by her father. Claudia and Frieda attempt to change the dynamics of the dichotomy of Pecola versus the community or outdoors versus a sense of spatial security. They try to impose order through their own blues expressiveness by speaking their magical "right words" over seeds planted in the black earth, in order to ensure that Pecola brings forth the life that would "bear witness" to an otherwise forgotten tragedy. Their magic fails, and remembrance of Pecola is left to Claudia's narrative recollection as text.

At the end of *The Bluest Eye* Claudia describes a pathetic picture of Pecola as a peculiar bird attempting to deliver herself from the bondage of walking upon the ground. Now completely insane, she is a hopeless spectacle. Claudia narrates:

> The damage done was total. She spent her days, her tendril, sap-green days walking up and down, her head jerking to the beat of a drummer so distant only she could hear. Elbows bent, hands on shoulders, she flailed her arms like a bird, in an eternal, grotesquely futile effort to fly. Beating the air, a winged but grounded bird, intent on the blue void it could not reach—could not even see—but which filled the valleys of the mind. (158)

The fragility of the gesture of flying without speed, wind, or anything more than arms for wings bespeaks the severity of her dementia. Yet there is something eerily lucid about her act. Pecola recognizes that she is constrained by the tyranny of place and of home (her family and her community) and unable to draw upon its resources. In contrast to the unforgiving apathy with which the ground confronts her, flight might possibly release her from the tyranny of place into an alternative reality. Despite the fact that Pecola understands that her groundedness is affiliated with her victimization, she does not comprehend any of the physical or metaphorical mechanics involved in achieving flight.

In *Corregidora* by Gayl Jones, this study of home will continue further inside than Morrison goes in *The Bluest Eye*. The body becomes the place of contention and the womb the crucial "black place." My concern, then, will shift from the physical site of kitchen places to the womb, or more precisely, the absence thereof. The novel suggests that the African American home ground must move away from the body to find room within the context of blues culture.

Notes

1. Doreen Massey, "Double Articulation: A Place in the World," in Angelika Bammer, ed., *Displacements: Cultural Identities in Question* (Bloomington: Indiana University Press, 1994), 110–21.

2. I share Lefebvre's emphasis on social space rather than a Lockean notion of "preexisting" space. I am concerned about the ways that people move in and through space/places.

3. Richard Wright, *Native Son* (New York: Bantam, 1940), 56.

4. Actually, the entire novel is an exploration of these experiences and nearly every character might be discussed in these terms. However, I am concerned here with the prominent kitchen sites that will offer a solid framework, if not all the gradations, for a discussion of home, blues, gender, race, and migration. For more comprehensive readings of *The Bluest Eye* see Madonne M. Minor, "Lady No Longer Sings the Blues: Rape, Madness, and Silence in *The Bluest Eye*" in Harold Bloom, ed., *Toni Morrison* (New York: Chelsea House, 1986), 85–99. Also Philip Page, *Dangerous Freedom: Fusion and Fragmentation in Toni Morrison's Novels* (Jackson: University Press of Mississippi, 1995); Ruth Rosenberg, "Seeds in Hard Ground: Black Girlhood in *The Bluest Eye*," *Black American Literature Forum* 21.4 (1987): 435–45; and Jane Somerville, "Idealized Beauty and the Denial of Love in Toni Morrison's *The Bluest Eye*," *Bulletin of the West Virginia Association of College English Teachers* 9.1 (1986): 18–23.

5. Unity and family are fundamental elements in the construction of home. In spatial terms, we can explore the significance of collectivities in the establishment of borders. Kathleen Kirby asserts that the establishment of place is directly related to how we are identified and what we are labeled (native or foreign, friend or foe, us or them). The act of delineating the boundary that distinguishes home from everything else necessarily includes the creation of a collectivity as well (this aspect of home and place making is explored more thoroughly in the next two chapters).

6. Mrs. Breedlove is given at least one warning when her tooth falls out. The narrator describes in some detail how the tooth could have been read as a sign and used to mount a resistance against a force like the tyranny of place. But Mrs. Breedlove does not act on this warning.

7. As in *Native Son*, the movies appear as a way for the larger society to promulgate its messages and to legitimize its authority. By refusing to depict anything other than black stereotypes, if it depicted African Americans in the movies at all, Hollywood helped distribute a racist discourse and value system.

8. This same point of confusion prompts one of Pecola's rare moments of blues expression while she is staying at the MacTeer household. "How do you get somebody to love you?" she asks Claudia and Frieda, as if she is repeating a classic blues refrain. The line is not so much a question to be answered, let alone by three little girls, as it is a line to be sung.

9. This novel is set in a period prior to the invention of colored contact lenses that could literally make brown eyes appear to have transformed to blue. The transformation, of course, would be affect rather than effect, so the underlying point of contestation would remain unresolved.

10. The green-and-white house depicted in the Dick and Jane reading primer is such a house. Morrison's point in offering this representation is to contrast the experiences of her various black characters with this image of a supposedly ideal, and harmless, home. See Chikwenye Okonjo Ogunyemi, "Order and Disorder in Toni Morrison's *The Bluest Eye*," *Critique: Studies in Modern Fiction* 19 (1977): 112–20.

11. We might even see how the blues idiom mediates on behalf of the prostitutes who live above the storefront. These women are not indicted by the self-righteousness of their neighbors; instead, their neighbors, in refusing to accept and to love Pecola, are indicted by them. See Denise Heinze, *The Dilemma of "Double Consciousness": Toni Morrison's Novels* (Athens: The University of Georgia Press, 1993).

Works Cited

Askeland, Lori. "Remodeling the Model Home in *Uncle Tom's Cabin* and *Beloved*." *American Literature* 64.4 (Dec. 1992): 795–805.

Awkward, Michael. *Inspiriting Influences: Tradition, Revision, and Afro-American Women's Novels*. New York: Columbia University Press, 1989.

Conner, Marc C. "From the Sublime to the Beautiful: The Aesthetic Progression of Toni Morrison." In Marc C. Conner, ed., *The Aesthetics of Toni Morrison: Speaking the Unspeakable*. Jackson: University Press of Mississippi, 2000, 49–76.

Franklin, Wayne and Michael Steiner, eds. "Taking Places: Toward the Regrounding of American Studies." In *Mapping American Culture*. Iowa City: University of Iowa Press, 1992, 3–23.

Grewal, Gurleen. *Circles of Sorrow, Lines of Struggle: The Novels of Toni Morrison*. Baton Rouge: Louisiana State University Press, 1998.

Hurston, Zora Neale. *Their Eyes Were Watching God*. New York: Harper and Row, 1937.

Johnson, Barbara. "'Aesthetic' and 'Rapport' in Toni Morrison's *Sula*." In Marc C. Conner, ed., *The Aesthetic of Toni Morrison: Speaking the Unspeakable*. Jackson: University Press of Mississippi, 2000, 3–11.

Kirby, Kathleen M. "Thinking Through the Body: The Politics of Location, Subjects, and Space." *Boundary* 2 20.2 (1993): 176.

Lefebvre, Henri. *The Production of Space*. Trans. Donald Nicholson-Smith. Cambridge: Blackwell Publishers Ltd., 1991.

McKittrick, Katherine. "'Black and 'Cause I'm Black I'm Blue': Transverse Racial Geographies in Toni Morrison's *The Bluest Eye*." *Gender Place and Culture: A Journal of Feminist Geography* 7.2 (June 2000): 125–43.

Morrison, Toni. *The Bluest Eye*. New York: Holt, Rinehart and Winston, 1970.

———. *Paradise*. New York: Knopf, 1998.

Moses, Cat. "The Blues Aesthetic in Toni Morrison's *The Bluest Eye*." *African American Review* 33 (Winter 99): 623–38.

Toomer, Jean. *Cane*. New York: Liveright, 1975.

Wong, Shelley. "Transgression as Poesis in *The Bluest Eye*." *Callaloo* 13.3 (Summer 1990): 471–81.

Wright, Richard. *12 Million Black Voices*. New York: Thunder's Mouth Press, 1941.

4

She's a Brick House: *Corregidora*

Although much has been written in the nearly twenty years since Houston A. Baker Jr. published *Blues, Ideology, and Afro-American Literature: A Vernacular Theory* (1984), his book offers a cogent place to begin discussion about home focused on *Corregidora*, by way of Toni Morrison's *Sula*. African American feminist scholars like Ann du Cille, Barbara Christian, Michael Awkward, and Deborah McDowell have critiqued Baker's work, in general, because of its sig-

She
rises from impulses of
hurt/to sing fine
print on the pain

—Sterling Plumpp, "Billie Holiday"

"Where did you get those songs?" . . .
"I made them up."

—Gayl Jones, *Corregidora*

A word is a bridge thrown between myself
and another.

—V. N. Volosinor, *Marxism and the Philosophy of Language*

nificant oversights and phallocentricism.[1] Even when Baker discusses purportedly symbolic aspects of literature, Ann du Cille argues, he tends to collapse the symbolic into the material at the expense of women. Writing about Baker's use of the Lacanian term "phallus" as a "signifier of the Father, or, better, of the Father's LAW," in his reading of *Invisible Man*'s Trueblood episode, du Cille suggests that Baker and Ellison both have "oversimplified" the fact that the "signifier and signified are not so easily separable." She continues, "For while the phallus may not be a material object, its action, its 'phallic energy,' its 'Father LAW' are not immaterial—certainly not to Matty Lou Trueblood, Pecola Breedlove, and other objects of its power" (448). Nevertheless, I return to *Blues Ideology*, in particular, because Baker's formulation of a blues matrix depends so heavily upon a metaphor drawn from the black female body. I do not mean to dismiss Baker's *Blues Ideology* as antifeminist, but neither am I willing to blindly apply his framework without offering a critique. Instead I am hoping to reclaim the matrix and to suggest ways to use the construct of home to expand upon the lexicon used for reading African American literature.

In chapter 1, "Living (Just Enough) for the City," and chapter 2, "Keep on Moving Don't Stop," the city is shown to circumscribe the experiences of "home" for the male protagonists, Bigger Thomas of *Native Son* and the narrator of *Invisible Man*. Ultimately, Bigger "can't win" against the austere façade of Chicago's Southside, and the invisible man cannot rest for running through the ever-changing face of Harlem. Neither can be "at home" in the Northern city—at least not for long. As limiting as home is for these characters, it is more so for Pecola Breedlove in *The Bluest Eye*. Home decreases from the (male) outdoor place of the city to the stultifying site of the black (female) indoor place of the kitchen. Nowhere is this reality more clearly demonstrated than in the tragic climax of the novel when Pecola is pinned bodily to the kitchen floor by the incestuous "embrace" of her father. Similarly, in Gayl Jones's *Corregidora*, the geographically limited space of kitchens, which shape Pecola's experiences of home, collapses into the even smaller site of the womb.

As illustrated in the previous chapter, "Get in the Kitchen and Rattle Them Pots and Pans," the spatial politics associated with the site of home in the novel shift from the indoor site of the kitchen to the quintessentially interior site represented by the pregnant figure of Pecola, who carries her father's dead seed. In its mapping of home, *Corregidora* follows a similar pattern, conflating kitchen and bedroom places that seem to lead inevitably to the womb.

In this chapter, I analyze Eva Peace from Toni Morrison's *Sula* and Catherine Lawson and Ursa from Gayl Jones's *Corregidora*. These characters, when read in succession, demonstrate the failure of the construct of Baker's "black hole," which is built upon the notion of a return to the womb, and show what is at stake for African American women at home. First, Eva becomes homicidal and kills her son when she perceives him as attempting to return to her as a "black hole." Then Catherine connects the physical place of home, specifically black, female-assigned places like the kitchen, with the black woman's body. Finally, Ursa's experiences as a producer of the blues culture Baker foregrounds reveal the dire price exacted from African American women in their attempt to overthrow the power dynamics imposed by the site of home.

Womb: A Black Hole

While Baker's *Blues Ideology* makes a significant contribution to the field of African American studies by utilizing the blues in literary analysis, his "matrix" reconfigures the blues as a womb, embodied in the metaphor of the "black (w)hole." But the body is the crucial aspect that the metaphor lacks. In Freudian terms, as Jane Gallop describes in *The Daughter's Seduction: Feminism and Psychoanalysis*, "Woman is then the figuration of phallic 'lack'; she is a hole" (22). Hazel Carby's critique of Du Bois's *The Souls of Black Folk* applies to Baker, who likewise "traces in its form, but displaces through its content, biological and sexual reproduction" (25). In his project, the woman has been discarded in favor of an asexual reproductive order that allows men to give birth to themselves. The man-made hole in *Blues Ideology* is given to do the work of the woman's body.

Nevertheless, a character like Ralph Ellison's nameless narrator of *Invisible Man* cannot simply fall underground, "into a home of sorts," and then, at the appropriate time, deliver himself fully actualized back into the world. Perhaps this is why we finally see him not reborn but trapped underground in a snapshot; he only appears to be in motion. The unsexed hole is neither a viable home place nor a place for rebirth. Instead, it can be described by Eva Peace's violent response to her son, Plum, in Morrison's *Sula*: "No!" she proclaims, "You can't be 'hole' and 'whole' at the same time." Eva kills Plum because, having come home from war addicted to drugs, he tries "to crawl back up into [her] womb." She discovers his need. He is not "whole" in any of its connotations.

In the following scene, Eva explains to her daughter, Hannah, why she killed Plum:

> It was such a carryin' on to get him born and to keep him alive. Just to keep his little heart beating and his little old lungs cleared and look like when he came back from that war he wanted to git back in. After all that carryin' on, just getting' him out and keepin' him alive, he wanted to crawl back in my womb and well. . . . I ain't got the room no more even if he could do it. . . . I couldn't do it again. . . . I would have let him if I'd've had the room but a big man can't be a baby all wrapped up inside his mamma no more; he suffocate. (71–72)

Eva adds rooms onto the house that took her years to build, so she is able to accommodate Plum *in her house*; but she has no room for him *in her home*, which she represents as womb. Here Morrison offers a more accurate representation of the power dynamics at work in Baker's black hole than any that Baker himself chooses in *Blues Ideology*. Like the protagonists in "Big Boy Leaves Home" and "The Man who Lived Underground" cited by Baker, Plum seeks a hole wherein he can escape the damaging effect of his experiences outside the black community. Having found that regenerative place, Baker suggests that these characters may reemerge whole at some time in the future. He envisions a model that would allow the male to utilize the reproductive power of a type of womb, but it does so by usurping the agency of the mother.

As Eva's son, perhaps Plum has a natural right to believe that if a place of healing and recovery exists for him, he will find it with his mother. From Eva's perspective, Plum imagines an idyllic return to wholeness, without seeming to be aware of its costs. Her response to Plum's effort to return home suggests that Eva is aware; in addition to the economic, emotional, and social costs, Eva would have to bear Plum's return bodily. Though he returns carelessly, in coming home Plum asserts the privilege of a man-child in a patriarchal society. But instead of seeing this gesture as natural, his mother reads his behavior symbolically. He has not simply come home; he is seeking to return to her womb. In this way, Eva is not just his biological mother. She becomes his ideological matrix. Plum seeks to disembody her to serve his own needs.

As Laura Doyle explains in *Bordering on the Body: The Racial Matrix in Modern Fiction and Culture*, kinship patriarchy is created by a dominant group of males who "control marriage in order to define and mythologize kin boundaries in a way that serves their needs as rulers" (25), and it is maintained at the expense of the woman who, as "mother," serves as the means through which men sustain their wealth, health, and control. "Not just psychologically but politically and aesthetically, then, the logic of kinship patriarchy turns a man against his kin source and leaves a woman to her own resources. The underlying problem, of course, begins when kinship patriarchy defines the mother as kin source" (27).

No matter how compelling Plum's needs may be, despite his desperate circumstances, Eva acts as if she can only give him what he desires at the expense of herself. Marianne Hirsch suggests, "In trying to explain to Hannah an act that is so obviously beyond comprehension, Eva dwells on an intense need for self-protection, a clear drawing of her own boundaries, a definitive expression of the limits of what she has to give, and she insists as well on Plum's boundaries, which, as a mother, she was forced to violate" (421). This seems contradictory since Eva repeatedly demonstrates her willingness to sacrifice herself on behalf of her children. After Boy Boy leaves she makes very difficult choices, the most legendary being the loss of her leg, which is rumored to have something to do with acquiring money for her starving family. Hirsch looks to this moment as the source of what she calls a "maternal discourse": "Eva's missing leg is the mark of maternal discourse in the novel and the key to its (thematized) ambivalence toward it" (419). Hirsch continues:

There is an ellipsis in the text, a silence surrounding Eva's eighteen-months' absence from Medallion. This gap gives rise to numerous tales, some told by Eva herself to amuse the children . . . others invented by the townspeople in their effort to explain her return without one leg, but with a new black pocketbook full of money. The tales are clearly apocryphal: The mother's (self-)mutilation in the service of her own and her children's survival remains, to the end of the novel, unnarrated, and perhaps unnarratable, but the source of endless narration. (419)

If we import Hirsch's argument into Baker's, the "maternal discourse" symbolized by the missing leg functions like a black hole within the text. The unspoken narrative becomes both the known origin and the mystery into which narrative attention is drawn. Not coincidentally, the moment that Hirsch points to in order to locate her "maternal discourse" is represented as an irresistible void, "the long fall of space below . . . [Eva's] left thigh" (31). Morrison builds her image of the maternal around the significant *something* that is missing. In its absence the leg becomes central; I agree with Hirsch's assessment that this absent something is central to the way that Eva functions as mother.

Of course, killing Plum comes with some emotional if not physical costs. What makes this different than any previous situation is the pressure exerted on Eva by Plum's desire to return home—since she is identified as that original home. Eva chooses to see herself as "whole" rather than to allow herself to be made into a "hole" into which he can climb. She makes the choice to be woman rather than womb. Unfortunately, Eva has a narrow perspective. Having thus limited her options, she is forced to make a *non*choice—to kill rather than be killed. Her "death" would come in the form of a transformation from woman to womb and would be symbolic; on the other hand, Plum's death is literally murder by his mother.

Eva refuses to distinguish between metaphor and reality. She is unwilling to bear the son, the child she fought so hard to keep alive, again. In her attempt to step outside the damaging gender dynamics of the black hole, she becomes alternately life-giver and destroyer. Hirsch argues that in *Sula* there is no escape from the "irresistible attraction" (to borrow Baker's language) of the construct of the maternal:

Holding on to a pervasive belief in the danger of the maternal, and reiterating that danger not only in the deaths of Chicken Little and of Plum, but also in the death of a large part of the town in the half-built, womblike tunnel at the end of the novel, the text demonstrates the trap that lies within the attempt to escape from the maternal. (426)

The problem lies in the metaphor. Once something goes into a black hole, it never comes out; not even light ever comes out again. In witnessing Eva's murder of her son, we learn in *Sula* what it takes four generations of women to discover in Gayl Jones's *Corregidora*: the dynamics of the black hole that privilege the womb over the woman must be dismantled, or the blues matrix will consume itself and threaten everything around it.

Kitchen: Mr. and Mrs. Hirshorn's Kitchen

The home Baker imagines is a womb without a woman; in *Corregidora* Gayl Jones tells the story of a woman struggling to be at home without a womb. The protagonist, Ursa Corregidora, has been given a directive passed down from her mother, grandmother, and great-grandmother—"make generations" in order to "bear witness" of past atrocities. The womb is the site her mothers insist she use as the means of bearing her (and their) experiences. Consequently, home becomes very local for Ursa. The women in this novel are sacrificed in favor of the womb and the men vilified in the name of the father.

The father in Ursa's home is Corregidora. Ursa represents the fourth generation of women to bear the name of the Portuguese Brazilian slave owner who prostituted his slaves. Her great-grandmother bore a daughter by him and this daughter, Ursa's grandmother, did too. The women keep the name Corregidora as a testament to this legacy of sexual domination and abuse. The boundaries of home for Ursa are constructed and maintained by a small (dying) community of women and still ruled by an absent father/lover. After her first husband, Mutt, causes her to fall down a flight of stairs, she is forced to have a hysterectomy. Ursa suddenly must confront a black hole, but a different one than Baker imagines. Rather than a womb, this black hole is the void left in place of her womb.

Ursa's uterus is rendered useless, and its premature fruit, a month-old fetus, is discarded. The womb, a most private and intensely personal place, becomes completely public when it is literally thrown away. This new black (female) public place supersedes the black hole and in so doing, makes room for Ursa to imagine an alternative home. She fills this new black (female) place with the blues. Unlike the previous discourse associated with home—"make generations"—the blues are necessarily social. Home shifts markedly from the perverse incestuous place that Ursa bears bodily to a site that is externalized and created in concert with others.

I begin my reading of this novel, however, not with Ursa but with Catherine Lawson. Although she is a minor character in the novel, Catherine's experiences are peculiarly black and female, and furthermore, they are characterized in terms of home. Catherine explicitly connects the built home with the black woman's body and moves us from Eva's resistance to the force exerted by the "black hole" (read as home) to Ursa's blues. Catherine provides the crucial insight that helps illuminate the dynamics at work in the material place of home, which seem to demand that any radical reconfiguration occur first in the material rather than the metaphorical realm—even if that material is a woman's body.

Catherine, called Cat, is not *at* home insofar as she has no assigned station that will afford her both liberty and humanity; instead, she struggles with being *not* home in the places where she lives and works. Cat struggles to explain to Ursa the relationship between her experiences at work, in Mr. and Mrs. Thomas Hirshorn's house, and her experiences at home. The recounting of those experiences allows us to import meaning into Ursa's similar confrontations with the place of home.

Catherine appears soon after the novel opens, bringing soup to Ursa during her recovery from the hysterectomy. She leaves town abruptly, soon after Ursa uncovers her lesbian relationship with Jeffy, the teenaged daughter of a friend. Cat is absent throughout the rest of the novel and only mentioned in Ursa's dreams and a passing conversation Ursa has on the street with an older Jeffy. Jeffy tells about a terrible accident involving Cat:

> She work over at the Wax Works, you know. One that makes Dixie Cups or something like that. She was reaching down to get something and got her hair caught in one of these machines and it pull all her hair out. Well, it pulled all the top part out. Might as well say all of it. She was in the hospital about six months. (176)

The relevance of this passage is obscured by its physical distance from a house, yet the forces at work in this scene are directly related to the power dynamics of home. As the older Jeffy states plainly in reference to the accident, "Bad thing to happen to a woman, ain't it?" (176). Long hair is a hallmark of womanhood and beauty. In this accident Jones quite deliberately represents "a bad thing" that happens "to a *woman*" [emphasis added] as opposed to a man. This *woman's* injury serves as blatant indication of those deeper scars that are more effectively concealed within Cat's past. At the beginning of the novel, she makes her living doing hair out of her kitchen. This affords her both economic means and the freedom "to keep [her] own hours" (29). For the time being, working out of her own home liberates Cat from the oppressive demands of the factory and the domestic work she used to perform. Unfortunately, she does not emerge from this past unscathed. In fact, by the end of the novel, she wears a bad wig in an effort to hide her disfigurement. Rather than functioning as a mask, the wig serves as a sign of the injury and reinforces the reality of Cat's debilitation.

The irony is that Cat knows employment in the factory is not very different from domestic work, in that black women's labor is exploited in order to serve the needs of white men and women.[2] Despite the fact that Cat's experiences, like Ursa's, are bound up with the blues, she seems to have no received cultural framework within which to express the value of her life. So instead, she replicates (and in so doing, falls victim to) the very systems of her oppression. Unable to utilize blues expressiveness, Cat tries in vain to explain her motivations to Ursa:

She was telling me about Mr. and Mrs. Thomas Hirshorn and something that happened in the kitchen . . . one morning he [Mr. Hirshorn] was sitting at the table while she was fixing coffee. "You pretty, Catherine, you know that? You pretty, Catherine. A lot of you nigger women is pretty." . . . He kept sitting, thumping on the table watching her . . . and then when she'd got the can of coffee grounds down and was opening it to pour it in the pot, he was behind her, touching her arm, and she dropped the can, and it banged and rolled across the kitchen floor spilling grains. (65)

In this scene, Jones lays out the black place of the kitchen as it has been constructed by the racialized, Southern past. Emancipation and the subsequent conditions leading to the Great Migration began dismantling the quarters and signaled the fall of Southern aristocracy. The kitchen is a "black" place in the ways that Jean Toomer describes in *Cane* in "Blood Burning Moon":

Bob Stone sauntered from his veranda out into the gloom of fir trees and magnolias. The clear white of his skin paled, and the flush of his cheeks turned purple. As if to balance this outer change, his mind became consciously a white man's. He passed the house with its huge open hearth which, in the days of slavery, was the plantation cookery. He saw Louisa bent over that hearth. He went in as a master should and took her. Direct, honest, bold. (31)

Bob Stone's prescribed place allows him free access to any and all sites within the plantation system. There are no limitations upon where and when he may enter any place—including Louisa's vagina. His actions are justified by the authority that deems Stone (as would-be master) *naturally* "direct," "honest," and "bold" in regard to Louisa (as would-be slave).

This passage makes explicit the fact that both terms, "hearth" and "home," are not only gendered but also racialized and as such, set within a matrix of power relationships. As Spillers explains:

"Gendering" takes place within the confines of the domestic, an essential metaphor that then spreads its tentacles for male and female subject over a wider ground of human and social purposes. Domesticity appears to gain its power by way of a common origin of cultural fictions that are grounded in the specificity of proper names, more exactly, a patronymic, which, in turn, situates those persons it "covers" in a particular place. (266)

Precisely because Cat is both black and female, she is assigned the role of domestic servant in a white family's kitchen. Consequently, her body as the signifier of that black female identity becomes the focal point. White male attention is directed toward her, and thus, her assigned place (the kitchen) and her experience of that place are expressed bodily.

Cat satisfies her need for control over her own home places by assuming a position of power over a young girl. She exercises that control according to the same despotic norms that have been used against her. Ursa overhears an exchange between Cat and Jeffy that demonstrates the dynamics:

> "If you bother [Ursa] again I'll give you a fist to fuck." . . .
> There was a loud slap, and then low crying.
> "Laugh now."
> "Please, Miss Catherine."
> "I said, 'Laugh now.'"
> Low crying. (47)

White patriarchy forced the black woman into the kitchen as domestic labor, then went further to dominate her body sexually. In response, Cat tries to move from the assigned black (female) "kitchen" place to invade and dominate Jeffy's womb. Cat justifies her lesbian relationship with this teenaged daughter of a friend who has been entrusted to her care by saying, "I wanted to come back home to my own bed and not be made a fool of. You know what I mean?" (66).

Early in the novel, Cat struggles to articulate her understanding in a way that might function as a mapping of her own as well as Ursa's experiences (at home). Cat clearly understands if she is ever to be *at* home, she must not be forced to stay in the kitchen. Referring to Ursa's employment as a blues singer, she tells her:

> You got talent. A talent or a craft, that's what I say, and don't have those sons of bitches hanging on your neck all the time. And daughters of bitches. When I was young I worked in white women's kitchens, so I know how it is. Leastwise the factory ain't a kitchen, but ain't much different. (29–30)

Ultimately, Cat is unable to successfully explain herself. In this way she operates as the foil who highlights the value of Ursa's contrasting experiences. Ursa's singing signifies off of Cat's experiences as a domestic worker and displaces her own would-be domestic experiences with the blues. However, Cat's experiences as a domestic should not be dismissed because they are intrinsically bound with Ursa's blues.[3]

The distance between the kitchen and the bedroom is compromised by the relatively unrestricted sexual appetite of Thomas Hirshorn, who sees Cat as simply an apparatus for feeding his hunger. She becomes, for him, an extension of the kitchen. As owner, Hirshorn can occupy Cat as territory almost as readily as he might eat the meal she prepares. In effect, the white man's response to her presence in *his* kitchen transforms the kitchen into a "bedroom" place.

The discursive walls that might be established by place to prohibit particular activities are absent within the racist aftermath of the slave economy. The owner of the house asserts his position of power over Cat through sexual harassment. She is forced to negotiate the slippery terrain that separates her livelihood from her "private" life while confronting a treacherous adversary. As her boss, Hirshorn has both the access and the power to make Cat "feel foolish all day in a white woman's kitchen" (64). Moreover, the experience is so destructive that it compromises the walls that might otherwise restrict "public" access to the "private" place of Cat's sexual body. The barriers that might distinguish the site of the kitchen from the site of the bedroom are obscured, and Cat's response is equally confused.

Through her relationship with Jeffy, Cat challenges the value she is assigned by the place of the kitchen and of the bedroom. Rather than acquiesce, she struggles to escape her designated place. Cat is seeking to reconfigure the nature of her own experience. In the effort, she becomes a "clumsy nigger" who is ultimately left a shadow of her former self, poorly masking her obvious disfigurement. Ursa, on the other hand, maps her journey home in the language of the blues.

Womb: Making Room

Jones uses Cat to demonstrate the material significance of kitchen places in the lives of African American women, but she underscores the quintessential blues paradigm at the heart of the novel. Ursa retains the paradoxical impulse to "make generations" even while she is left wombless by her fall. The patriarch Corregidora rejects even the façade of the kitchen in favor of the bedroom and capitalizes on black women's bodies as sexual commodities. The mothers dispute this relationship first by trying to assert their humanity, then by refusing to allow the testament to Corregidora's inhumanity to die.

Unfortunately, they co-opt the womb as a site for domination and, instead of liberating themselves, thus risk reifying the terms of their oppression. Amy Gottfried considers the ironic implications of their response: "The Corregidora women respond to their early enslavement by defining themselves and their daughters as wombs intended for the literal bearing of witnesses. Sexual violence doubly limits desire and pleasure for these women. First defined as 'pussy,' they are now self-defined as womb" (560). Trying to liberate herself from Corregidora, Great Gram sought to make a home for herself and her daughters. She moves from her distinctly black (female) would-be kitchen/bedroom place as "little gold piece" in Brazil to her womb in Kentucky as an attempt to control the productivity of her own body.

By Ursa's time, however, Great Gram's desire to control her own body serves as a mandate for Ursa and her mother, Correy. The question they grapple with over the course of the novel is whether or not the position depicted by Corregidora is any better than the one Great Gram and Gram actually held.[4] Ursa's journey home must move her away from the kitchen as well as from the womb.

In "Mama's Baby," Spillers evokes the image of the Mother within the context of African America. In contrast to the symbolic realm overshadowed, in the Lacanian view, by the specter of the Father, here the Father is absent by design. While Lacan suggests that the Father is always in doubt, from Spillers's perspective, he is both doubted and denied, and the offspring are given over to the "condition of the mother." Such a shift requires more than a simple reading of race and gender and evokes a complicated lexicon upon which we might build a vocabulary for literary analysis.

The Corregidora women attempt to invert the pastoral image of home by insisting that the father is the source of their kin, and their black female bodies testify to the sins of his house. The quest is not to achieve regeneration, as for Plum in *Sula,* but to pass on the legacy of Corregidora. As H. A. Ashraf notes:

> In Ursa's memories of Great Gram's slave heritage, there's no ambivalence (since Great Gram had ensured that there would be no questioning her version of the past), no paradoxes since the tale is of pure victimage and equally pure evil, and little feeling that Ursa was supposed to be searching for her own identity at all. The ghosts are not being exorcised; they're being embalmed. (276)

Ashraf borrows an image from Salman Rushdie of a haunting, but it is the women themselves who are haunted.[5] Ursa is charged to "make generations" in order to pass down the legacy as it was told to her: Corregidora is the incontestable paternal figure who shamelessly harbored Great Gram and Gram as property—his "little gold piece"—and sexual chattel.[6]

Ursa understands enough about this legacy to reject kitchen places and to seek a more viable home place. She chooses the stage as the place to begin the arduous journey away from Corregidora's memory toward her own home, created through the blues. On the blues performer's stage, female bodies are both liberated through the reduction of incomprehensibly painful experiences into manageable terms and policed by the intervening presence of mothers and men. Yet the stage is not the site of Ursa's tragedy. She is knocked down a flight of stairs by her drunken husband on her way home after an evening performance. Ursa's fall marks the violent flashpoint when all the dynamics of place making come together within the text.

On the surface, Mutt is angry about Ursa's occupation because her performances arouse other men. He threatens her: "'That's what I'm gon do,' he said. He was standing with his arms all up in the air. I was on my way to work. 'One a y'all wont to bid for her? Piece a ass for sale. . . . That's what y'all wont, ain't it? Piece a ass'" (159). In isolation, Mutt's actions might read as a domineering man trying to control his wife's interactions. However, when read in the context of history as well as the Corregidora women's quest to "make generations," they reveal a more complicated dynamic at work.

While the kitchen collapsed into the bedroom for many black women, Corregidora was only invested in the latter. Great Gram's assigned place within the Brazilian household was as a concubine— his "little gold piece." In the tradition established by Great Gram, Ursa tries to walk away from her black (female) home place. But she is not completely liberated from the kitchen/bedroom dynamic simply because she resists it. The Corregidora women are subject to the force exerted by the larger construct of home. So when Ursa is ultimately scarred by place, it is as the result of a fall down a flight of stairs, a liminal place between the stage—the home of Ursa's choosing—and the assigned black (female) kitchen and bedroom.

The Corregidora women use their bodies to establish a place for themselves secure enough to withstand Corregidora's dominion. Unfortunately, as Gottfried asserts, "Sexual commodification is supplanted by a deliberate, political self-definition. But as Ursa . . . discovers, this political move has a double-edged drawback: The Corregidoras' agenda severely limits their sexual identities, a limitation which in turn provokes domestic violence" (559). Like Ursa, Mutt is trying to secure a home for himself, and he responds violently to the perceived threat to it by transforming the site of Ursa's body. In the process, Ursa loses her womb[7]—the place that had been configured as the enduring site of the Corregidora legacy. The absence of her uterus becomes a *"well that never bleeds"* (99). This black hole contains neither water nor blood with which to sustain life. In Ursa's imagination she hears Mutt say to her, *"Let me get up in your hole, I said. I wont to get up in your goddamn hole"* (100). Mutt transforms the quintessential *something* embodied by Ursa's womb into a void. In so doing, he physically expresses his desire to enter the place that was occupied by Ursa's womb; once again, as with Eva and Plum, home is imagined in these terms.[8]

Although she resists mystifying the material site of home, at the end of the story when Mutt finally reenters her life, Ursa is drawn back to the specific place where they lived, presumably in the hope of rectifying past mistakes. The last pages of the novel offer a hope not present anywhere else, because at this moment language intersects with body, place, and memory as both Mutt and Ursa articulate what they want and need on their own terms:

> A moment of pleasure and excruciating pain at the same time, a moment of broken skin but not sexlessness. . . . I held his ankles. It was like I didn't know how much was me and Mutt and how much was Great Gram and Corregidora. . . .
>
> "I could kill you."
>
> He came and I swallowed. He leaned back, pulling me up by the shoulders.
>
> "I don't want a kind of woman that hurt you," he said.
>
> "Then you don't want me."
>
> "I don't want a kind of woman that hurt you."
>
> "Then you don't want me."
>
> "I don't want a kind of woman that hurt you."
>
> "Then you don't want me."
>
> He shook me till I fell against him crying. "I don't want a kind of man that'll hurt me neither," I said. He held me tight. (184–85)

Ursa's epiphany comes at the end of the novel, when she finally understands that in order to construct a viable home place, she must shift the emphasis, bodily, from "the well which never bleeds"—its life-giving, and more important, life-sustaining powers all inarguably gone—to her mouth, the site that permits the expression of her blues. The difficulty as well as the deliberateness of this shift is emphasized by her concluding posture. Certainly, the novel ends ambiguously. But in its last pages, Ursa successfully integrates the past into what Deborah McDowell calls a "continuous present"[9] that allows her finally to imagine a home built out of her experiences as well as those of her foremothers, Corregidora, and Mutt.

Much has been said about the concluding lines of *Corregidora* as a blues exchange.[10] The blues, of course, have been associated with both movement and the translation of experiences into alternative terms. They permit disparate experiences to converge at a single moment in time and so facilitate Ursa's epiphany. The suffocating site of the womb needs to be discarded, the novel suggests, in favor of a less "totalizing" narrative, to borrow language from Michel de Certeau.[11] The concluding blues song Ursa sings with Mutt is "jerry-built" from fragments of the past. The blues narrative produced in place of the womb opens up room for maneuvering outside the stultifying interior site configured by Great Gram and Corregidora.

The integrity of the structural blueprint introduced in *Native Son* and revised by Ellison in *Invisible Man* and Morrison in *The Bluest Eye* is threatened by complete collapse in *Corregidora*. Jones begins her demolition with the womb, but by the end of the novel, even the blues Ursa sings is compromised. In *Song of Solomon,* Morrison will recover the patronym and collect the remnants of the city, the kitchen, and the womb to reconstruct the African American place of home. Finally, in this novel, we find a representation of home, not without contradictions or completely unproblematic, but with enough conflict resolved that we can imagine laying down our bones to rest for a while.

Notes

1. The 1980s and '90s were the backdrop for much infighting between women seeking to validate literary representations of their experiences at home and men seeking control over the master's tongue and house. Alice

Walker's search for Zora Neale Hurston's grave took her to her "mother's house." As a result of her efforts and those of many others before her, African American female authors like Margaret Walker, Gwendolyn Brooks, Toni Morrison, Octavia Butler, Gloria Naylor, Ntozake Shange, Toni Cade Bambara, and Gayl Jones rose to dominate the field of fiction writing. However, men sought a home of a different sort within the house of the academy. Into the twenty-first century, the most renowned criticism and theory continue to be produced by men like Henry Louis Gates Jr. and Houston A. Baker Jr. Such a reality does not suggest an inherently divided house that opposes "writers" and "readers"; nonetheless, it seems a disparity between "writing" and "reading" arose along gender lines.

2. White Americans read the presence of African American domestic workers as a sign of their own domestic security. Nearly a hundred years after the collapse of the slave economy, home for white people continued to be stabilized at the expense of black laborers (even if much of the "stabilizing" was more symbolic than actual labor). For this reason, African American women had few employment opportunities besides domestic work. Home is invented in a contest for power from which someone will emerge victorious and someone will invariably lose. Domestic service is but a by-product of this struggle.

3. Lindon Barrett makes this connection between domestic service and the blues explicit in his reading of a scene from Billie Holiday's autobiography. Despite the questions of authenticity that have been raised in relationship to this work, his discussion is relevant not only because Holiday (as character if not historical person) writes about her experiences of black (female) places as a domestic worker who employs relevant cartographical strategies, but also because, like the fictional Ursa, "the lady sings the blues." Barrett's discussion is in reference to the following scene he cites from Holiday's autobiography, *Lady Sings the Blues*:

> All these bitches were lazy. I knew it and that's where I had them. They didn't care how filthy their damn houses were inside, as long as those white steps were clean. Sometimes I'd bring home as much as ninety cents a day. I even made high as $2.10—that's fourteen kitchen or bathroom floors and as many sets of steps.

It is [Holiday's] "originary" labor that affirms the site (sight) of the valued and the not-valued, the inside and the outside; it is her antinominan presence on the boundary and, finally, within the house—primarily kitchens and bathrooms, architectural sites of inside meeting outside—

that maintains the value of the valued. Insofar as Holiday is outside, the low, down, dirty, maid, the commanded, the not-valued, she is a source of value. . . . (874)

Holiday is housed insofar as she stays put, in those built places that require the services of black females—steps, kitchens, bathrooms. Yet, as Barrett suggests, designations such as "high" versus "low," "rich" versus "poor," "dirty" versus "clean" are relative rather than essential. Holiday gains a level of control over these home places by reformulating the terms of her oppression. She literally rewrites them through the language of autobiography and the blues. In the passage from *Lady Sings the Blues*, Holiday curses the women and calls them "nasty." The white women whose homes she works in become "dirty" while she, by implication, is clean. See "'In the Dark': Billie Holiday and Some Sights and Sounds of American Value," *Callaloo* 13.4 (1990): 872–85.

Leon Forrest also connects a discussion about Billie Holiday with *Corregidora* in his article "A Solo Long-Song: For Lady Day" in *Callaloo* 16.2 (Spring 1993): 332–67. Forrest writes, "The mythical power of Billie Holiday's life, charged by the immediate abuse from men throughout her life, and the mythical-sexual victimization by the slave master of her great grandmother becomes an obvious scale-model for a most troubling and memorable novel *Corregidora*, by Gayl Jones" (364).

4. Nancy Jesser makes the following observation in her insightful reading of Toni Morrison's *Beloved*: "The specificity of historical moments allows for and demands certain and, at times, mixed-up choices. None are choices for all time, and none are apocalyptic enough to end the history in which we find ourselves. But, Morrison suggests [in *Beloved*], we bear a kind of haunting from these choices that in turn haunts the future" (341). The house in Bracktown is haunted with ghosts of her mother's past, and Ursa must leave in order to begin her *own* journey toward "home." See Nancy Jesser, "Violence, Home and Community in Toni Morrison's *Beloved*," *African American Review* 33.2 (Summer 1999): 325–45.

5. From the start of the novel, Ursa's sense of place grows primarily from two directions: from the demand that she "make generations" in order to record past atrocities, as she literally has been born to do; and out of her desire to sing the blues. I do not mean to suggest that the command to "make generations" and the blues are divergent. In fact, at times they are nearly synonymous. Once we also consider the conditions that lead to Ursa's hysterectomy, we have the necessary tensions established to nurture the

blues. A black woman's encounter with her assigned place, either in the kitchen (ultimately pinned to the floor by her father, as Pecola is in *The Bluest Eye*) or on the steps (like Pauline Breedlove ordering meaningless things or Billie Holiday polishing white marble) or in the factory (as Cat comes to be), ends with her wearing the scars of her experiences bodily.

6. In her reading of *Beloved*, Doyle makes an observation that is relevant to this discussion:

> Like the white men who steal Sethe's milk in Toni Morrison's *Beloved*, dominant-group men drink the milk that would nourish the cultural expressions of subordinate-group men. As Halle dramatizes, this theft renders the men emotionally numb and strikes them symbolically deaf and dumb. Meanwhile the theft of literal and metaphorical milk leaves the women to create a "told story" out of nothing but their own scarred and sequestered bodies. In fact, all women who would be artists, whether they belong to dominant or subordinate kin groups, must struggle to de-symbolize themselves, which they often begin to do by withdrawing, either voluntarily or involuntarily, from the marriage circuit. (26–27)

Certainly we see this pattern reflected in *Corregidora* where, in her struggle to forge a place for herself, Ursa is forced from both marriage and reproduction.

7. Mutt's perverse response to Ursa, in knocking her down a flight of steps, is similar to Paul D's encounter with the ghost in *Beloved*. As Nancy Jesser observes in her reading of the novel, "[Paul D's] coming [to 124 Bluestone Road] disrupts the physical spaces of the house. He 'broke up the place, making room, shifting [the ghost], moving it over to someplace else, then standing in the place that he had made'" (338). See Nancy Jesser, "Violence, Home, and Community in Toni Morrison's *Beloved*," *African American Review* 33.2 (Summer 1999): 325–45.

8. Deborah McDowell, "Negotiating Between the Tenses: Witnessing Slavery After Freedom—*Dessa Rose*," in Deborah E. McDowell and Arnold Rampersad, eds., *Slavery and the Literary Imagination* (Baltimore: Johns Hopkins University Press, 1989), 144–63.

9. See Katherine Boutry, "Black and Blue: The Female Body of Blues Writing in Jean Toomer, Toni Morrison, and Gayl Jones," in Saadi A. Simawe, ed., *Black Orpheus: Music in African American Fiction From the Harlem Renaissance to Toni Morrison* (New York: Garland, 2000), 91–118; Melvin Dixon, *Singing a Deep Song: Language as Evidence in the Novels of Gayl Jones* (Garden City, NY: Anchor-Doubleday, 1984), 236–48; Gunilla T.

Kester, "The Blues, Healing, and Cultural Representation in Contemporary African American Women's Literature," in Lilian Furst, ed., *Women Healers and Physicians: Climbing a Long Hill* (Lexington: University Press of Kentucky, 1997), 114–27; and Claudia Tate, "*Corregidora*: Ursa's Blues Medley," *Black American Literature Forum* 13 (1979): 139–41.

10. In *The Practice of Everyday Life*, trans. Steven Rendall (Berkeley: University of California Press, 1984), Michel de Certeau theorizes that: "For the technological system [embodied by the city] of a coherent and totalizing space that is 'linked' and simultaneous, the figures of pedestrian rhetoric substitute trajectories that have a mythical structure . . . [for] a story jerry-built out of elements taken from common sayings, an allusive and fragmentary story whose gaps mesh with the social practices it symbolizes" (102).

Works Cited

Ashraf, H. A. "'Relate Sexual to Historical': Race, Resistance, and Desire in Gayl Jones's *Corregidora*." *African American Review* 34 (2) (2000): 273–297.

Baker, Houston A. *Blues, Ideology, and Afro-American Literature: A Vernacular Theory*. Chicago: University of Chicago Press, 1984.

Carby, Hazel. *Race Men*. Cambridge: Harvard University Press, 1998.

Doyle, Laura. *Bordering on the Body: The Racial Matrix of Modern Fiction and Culture*. New York: Oxford University Press, 1994.

du Cille, Ann. "Phallus(ies) of Interpretation." In Winston Napier, ed., *African American Literary Theory*. New York: New York University Press, 2000, 443–59.

Gallop, Jane. *The Daughter's Seduction: Feminism and Psychoanalysis*. Ithaca: Cornell University Press, 1982.

Gottfried, Amy S. "Angry Arts: Silence, Speech, and Song in Gayl Jones's *Corregidora*." *African American Review* 28 (4) (1994): 559–70.

Hirsch, Marianne. "Maternal Narratives: 'Cruel Enough to Stop the Blood.'" In Henry Louis Gates Jr., ed., *Reading Black, Reading Feminist: A Critical Anthology*. New York: Meridian, 1990.

Jones, Gayl. *Corregidora*. Boston: Beacon, 1975.

Morrison, Toni. *Sula*. New York: Knopf, 1973.

Spillers, Hortense J. "Mama's Baby, Papa's Maybe: An American Grammar Book." In Winston Napier, ed., *African American Literary Theory: A Reader*. New York: New York University Press, 1990, 257–79.

Toomer, Jean. *Cane*. New York: Liveright, 1975.

[Home is] *this* world, the world of which we
are normally aware . . . the social setting in
which man may expect to find his secure
place. [The unhomely, t]hat which is 'secret',
and that which usually remains hidden but
is brought to light, is the unconscious mind
of the individual, and through and beyond this
is a wider region of the unconscious that we
find embodied in myths, legends and fairy
tales throughout the world; it is the realm of
primitive fears, of what has been forgotten and
left behind, yet returns on occasions to plague
us; it is the sense of alienation, of things we
have made turning against us, of historical
and social forces that we are helping to shape
and that yet escape our control and even our
knowledge; and it may also be a sense of the
'wholly other' invading our lives.

—Siegbert S. Prawer, "The 'Uncanny' in Literature"

Europeans living in America have undergone
a transformation. [Carl] Jung calls this process
"going Black."

—Ishmael Reed, *Mumbo Jumbo*

5

God Bless the Child That's Got His Own: *Song of Solomon*

In *Mumbo Jumbo* (1972), Ishmael Reed muses about the possibility of "blackness" sweeping the country like a contagion of pandemic proportions. Reed suggests that during the 1920s, inspired by the rhythms of black cultural productions, the United States succumbed to its urge to jelly roll, betraying its white façade by exposing its dark underbelly. In this satire, Reed paints a picture of a nightmarish plague that the establishment is unable to quell.

The infestation is not, however, a foreign agent introduced to a virgin population. Instead, the phenomenon arises from inside the nation. It is a repressed part of our national identity manifested as blues, ragtime, jazz, returning to seize control of the dominant consciousness. The "alien" black presence so vital to building and maintaining the nation, in Reed's vision, spreads beyond white supremacist stopgaps and Jes Grew out of control. Funk infests the country and alters its pulse to match the rhythm of the soft-shoe that reveals more than a trace of resemblance to the African foot stomp upon bare ground. Without regard for accepted norms and practices, people began to show their color; otherwise "good" people began to "act black" in their style of dress, music, speech, and performance.

For a time, Jes Grew emerged from the recesses of our consciousness and proved itself a crucial part of our national identity. In this parody, Reed shows what is at stake for a country and a people still struggling to define itself as home for African Americans only a few generations removed from slavery. Even the suggestion that Jes Grew's elusive Text ever existed challenges ontological beliefs about racial divisions within society. Such categories are not hermetic. The distinctions between communities were becoming increasingly difficult to identify by the tracks that had previously separated them. Reed's notion of Jes Grew is important because knowing *where* we are cartographically relies upon knowing *who* we are as a people. These, of course, are not new questions, and they continue to permeate the writings of successive generations at least in part because they are so difficult to answer.

Reed's critique and his reference to Jung's observation about the European American "going Black" provide a convenient metaphor upon which to anchor the concept of home. American national identity is founded upon formulations of race. Consequently, we utilize the language of race to help us articulate the ways in which we inhabit the land. As a result, home is built upon metaphors of racial identity. But what might appear at a great distance to be simply black and white becomes infinitely complicated the more closely it is examined.

While not overtly concerned with addressing the needs of a white audience in the ways reflected in Reed's *Mumbo Jumbo*, Toni Morrison creates an unapologetically black home place that nevertheless manages to demonstrate a sophisticated understanding of race. The natural world of borders—walls, fences, streets, streams, and mountains—that define home in *Song of Solomon* is accompanied by the ghettoized world of breast milk, bones, peaches, blues, and ghosts. Unfortunately, the credence lent to the world of borders by the authority of maps, government agencies, and other institutions usually occludes the significance of the ghetto.

The ghetto is, of course, a portion of the city assigned to disenfranchised members of society who generally share a common racial identity. But in the African American vernacular, "ghetto" is also a characterization for something or someone, or an act or behavior that is identified with the place of the ghetto. It is both a particular material site identified in terms of spatial markers like street signs and housing projects and the more arbitrary label assigned to nearly anything "black" that might be associated with that locale. To be "ghetto" is to act flagrantly out of one's impulses in spite of the presence of strangers. For example, in *Song of Solomon*, Porter's public display of drunkenness, shouting and urinating out of an attic window, might be called "ghetto."

In *Song of Solomon*, the city itself becomes "ghetto"—not in the sense of Bigger Thomas's segregated and impoverished Southside, which he knows intimately but which refuses to know him, nor in the sense that *Invisible Man*'s Harlem is a black jungle that keeps slipping out of view. I do not want to dismiss the standard usage of the term; obviously, the word "ghetto" denotes slums African Americans were forced by economic pressures to occupy. What I am suggesting, however, is that in its standard usage the term is pejorative; the derivative from the vernacular includes this connotation but is inflected with a broader meaning. These black cities can barely house the protagonists and are not home to them. To be "ghetto" in the vernacular sense is to have a home even if it is an illegitimate nonplace that emerges alongside that which appears to be more natural. *Song of Solomon*'s Southside, for example, is ghetto because it is the dark underbelly that is home to the characters' blacker selves.

In this chapter I will examine the ways in which Morrison signifies on the leitmotif of the earlier novels and reconfigures the places of the city, the kitchen, and the womb in terms that are more livable. The representation of home, drawn as an irresistible attraction toward increasingly smaller sites—the city, the kitchen, the womb—in the previous works, breaks free and explodes in *Corregidora*. Morrison gathers the pieces Jones scatters and in *Song of Solomon* inverts the pattern, leading us out of the womb rather than into it. The womb is dead; the kitchen opens outward; and the city becomes ghetto. Rather than being a black place because it is so interior that there is an absence of light, as is the case with Baker's black hole, home becomes a black place because of the presence of all color. To be at home, then, Morrison suggests in *Song of Solomon*, the African American community must embody the blues paradox of holding its opposite within itself. The novel declares that home is untenable, yet it must be defended even at the cost of life itself. The protagonist, Milkman, having gained the knowledge of how to integrate the material world embodied by his father with the ghetto symbolized by his aunt, can finally fly home.

Womb: A Dead Place

While Baker's theoretical framework in *Blues Ideology* erases the mother by subjugating the productive space of the biological womb to the male-engineered matrix, *Song of Solomon* resists such a reading by privileging the woman's body. Although the womb is clearly a hostile place that can be invaded by potentially lethal forces, Morrison refuses to let the reader forget that the womb is located within a woman's body. She creates dynamic characters with individual personalities not easily ignored, even when the novel moves from the literal womb into metaphor. In *Song of Solomon,* representations of the womb are repeated and revised in a range that spans the mythical, the literal, and the metaphorical. The most obvious example of a mythical womb is, of course, Pilate's emergence from Sing's dead womb. Milkman's life is literally threatened when he is still in Ruth's womb, and as an adult he helps to destroy Hagar's barren womb. Finally, the novel offers the Butlers' house as a metaphor for a decaying womb through which Milkman reconnects with his ancestral past.

Although much has been written about Pilate's mythic origins, I return to this point because her birth is a clear demonstration of Morrison's concern for the womb as it relates to the quest for home. Even Pilate's brother, Macon Dead II, who, in his pursuit of material gain, has become estranged from his sister and detached from his ancestry, recognizes Pilate's link to the past. He tells his son, Milkman, "If you ever have a doubt we from Africa, look at Pilate" (54). She represents the African who was wrested from her homeland only to be denied the liberty of establishing a home in the new land. The struggle in the novel to acquire an estate to pass on to future generations is similar to the contest depicted in *Corregidora* to "make generations" that "bear witness" of the past. In an attempt to liberate Ursa from the perverse dogma instituted by her great-grandmother, Jones literally cuts the womb out of the woman's body. However problematically, the hysterectomy and its precipitating violence free Ursa from the cycle of maternity and allow her to withdraw from the marriage circuit in an effort to redefine her relationship to home. The womb and fetus lost in *Corregidora* are reclaimed in *Song of Solomon*. While Ursa's fetus is premature and discarded along with the womb, Sing's baby matures to full term.

Morrison understands the need to reconfigure the role the female body plays in the African American construction of home. The novels discussed in the previous chapters become increasingly critical of the effort to retreat into the womb. Morrison revises Jones's violent dismemberment, which radically alters the place of Ursa's body, by keeping the womb intact even while insisting that it not be considered a viable home. Morrison accomplishes this by allowing the woman to choose death over the responsibilities of motherhood. Pilate declares, "People die when they want to and if they want to" (141). Unfortunately, in choosing to die *before* Pilate is born, Sing literally holds the future captive in her womb. Pilate's sheer determination to live overcomes death. She delivers herself from the cavern of dead flesh that might have been her tomb.

In this birth, Morrison posits a paradox that is characteristic of the blues expression that will come to shape Pilate's life. Pilate embodies the blues sentiment expressed by lyrics like "Sometimes I feel like a motherless child," growing out of the slave past. Slave families were torn apart and children routinely denied a relationship with their mothers. This terrible reality is supported, perhaps ironically, by an equally heinous law supporting the institution of slavery, which mandated that children "follow the condition of the mother." This law in conjunction with governing practices functioned to erode the natural right of a black individual to control access to her own body and her offspring. In "Mama's Baby," Spillers maintains that "Under these arrangements, the customary lexis of sexuality, including 'reproduction,' 'motherhood,' 'pleasure,' and 'desire' are thrown into unrelieved crisis" (272). I have already discussed at some length how the blues emerges from this troubled past and works to impose meaning upon the chaos of black experiences. In fact, the blues is one of the few narrative traditions that can accommodate the hyperbole and truth, hope and angst, of a mother who dies *before* the child is even born. Sing's womb, then, is a blues crossing, that black (female) place Baker might call a "black hole." Pilate must overcome the condition of her mother— and her own quintessential blues condition of being a motherless child—before she can claim the right to be alive.

The black hole that Baker describes is indicated by the X, the sign of the railway juncture. The X, however, evokes the image of America's mechanization and thus diverts attention from the female body. However, Pilate emerges from her mother's dead womb bearing no mark of this crossing at all. The narrative describes the scene of Pilate's birth from Macon's perspective:

> After their mother died, she had come struggling out of the womb without help from throbbing muscles or the pressure of swift womb water. As a result, for all the years he knew her, her stomach was smooth and stur-

dy as her back, at no point interrupted by a navel. It was the absence of a navel that convinced people she had not arrived through normal channels. . . . Once the new baby's lifeline was cut, the cord stump shriveled, fell off, and left no trace of having ever existed. (27–28)

The absence of a navel suggests the polar opposite of Baker's junction. Pilate's smooth belly brings to mind anything but the man-made. The absence of a navel bears witness to her mother's death, but it also indicates an unnatural break with the past. Morrison moves toward resolving the dilemma of the absent mother by reinscribing her in Pilate's flesh as the absence of a navel. Pilate is *un*marked by her mother's death. Like Adam, who as the first man has no need for a navel, Pilate with her smooth belly signifies originality. Further, she is given dominion over the tools that will reconnect the next generation with its past. This heritage transcends the black hole of her mother's womb and reaches beyond the vortex of the Middle Passage to an African past. Consequently, that "captive flesh," which had been "seared, divided, ripped-apart . . . riveted to the ship's hole, fallen, or escaped overboard" (Spillers 260) in the ancestral past, is permitted to begin again. In this way, Pilate's belly becomes a blues paradigm simultaneously signifying the problem and the solution.

Morrison reinforces the idea that the womb is a hostile place through the figures of Macon's wife, Ruth, and Pilate's granddaughter, Hagar. These women desperately long for a viable home that will nurture their embattled psyches. The devaluation of the womb corresponds with the dynamics established by their respective homes: Ruth's is too big and Hagar's is too detached. As a result, the womb again emerges as a sign of home and its dysfunction.

Ruth is the lonely daughter of the first African American doctor in town. She never discovers any meaningful ways of expressing herself in the overwhelmingly masculinist space of Not Doctor Street and her father's house. Southside residents integrate the doctor's home into their cultural landscape but they do not accommodate Ruth; and the house that justifies the expanded reading of African American space for the community at large collapses in upon his daughter. Without a sense of ownership, Ruth *belongs* to the house. Consequently, the social space that might read as an expanded site of power for the African American community in general, Ruth finds nearly impossible to negotiate. As Lefebvre explains, "The subject experiences space as an obstacle, as a resistant objectality: at times as implacably hard as a concrete wall, being not only extremely difficult to modify in any way but also hedged about by Draconian rules prohibiting any attempt at such modification" (57). Because the house is expansive, it seems available to be encoded at will, but instead of yielding itself as a void, it refuses to be fitted to Ruth's female sensibilities. Her efforts to resist the sense of smallness her home imposes upon her are ineffectual and usually result in negligible changes in her mundane routine. The birth of her son, Milkman, is her only significant victory over the conditions that shape her life.

Nevertheless, Ruth would not have been able to conceive Milkman without Pilate's assistance. Pilate arrives in town after discovering that her granddaughter, Hagar, is not like her daughter, Reba, or herself. Hagar's appetites cannot be satiated by wandering. She needs a home, so Pilate seeks to reconnect with her more conventional brother. The reunion is brief, just longer than the time it takes Milkman to grow from conception to birth. When Macon discovers that Ruth is pregnant, he initiates a regimen designed to induce an abortion. While Milkman has not yet become "real" to her, Ruth is terrified by the possibility of aborting the fetus. Nevertheless, she is unable to resist her husband and submits to castor oil, scalding pots, soapy enemas, and knitting needles. When he punches her in the stomach, she finally looks to Pilate for help.

For Ruth, the womb is not a haven; nor is it perverted into a record through which she can "bear witness" of the past. With Pilate's assistance, Ruth asserts the sovereign right to control access to her body. Her womb, under siege by Macon, characterizes the struggle of African American women to liberate themselves from oppressive domestic dogma that seems to extend the reach of male governance to the female body. When paired with Pilate, Ruth no longer serves as the malleable conduit for expanding and maintaining male territory. Rather than functioning as a mere kin source, Ruth begins to exercise dominion over her life and affect the lives of others. She manipulates Macon into impregnating her and she manages to resist his threats long enough for her son to be born.

Within a larger context, *Song of Solomon* contains none of the nostalgia associated with Ruth, as mother, found in some of the earlier literature. For example, we cannot imagine Milkman running and jumping over puddles of milk to get to Ruth in the way the narrator does in his attempt to get to Mary Rambo in *Invisible Man*. The dark hole into which the invisible man falls during the Harlem riots is a surrogate for Mary Rambo's body. The basement apartment is simply an extension of this same association. The apartment reads as Baker's matrix, a womblike blues home wherein the narrator can withdraw from his experiences in the world. Morrison reconfigures Ellison's vocabulary—man, milk, mother, home, and womb—and inflects the terms with new meaning. Milkman's experiences quell the optimism associated with a retreat into the womb. The womb, in *Song of Solomon*, does not bear even the trace of romance. For Milkman, home must be a broader place, located elsewhere. The womb is not safe for Milkman as it was not safe for Pilate.

Pilate says that Milkman "come into the world tryin to keep from getting killed" (140); but this reality seems to have made him selfish. He treats Pilate's hungry granddaughter, Hagar, with the same callous disregard his father gives his mother. Ultimately, Hagar drowns in a pool of her own longings, manifested as a mad desire for Milkman. Though he falls in love with Hagar the moment he sees her, over the course of time his lust wanes; meanwhile, her passion for him becomes more concentrated. Although the bodily consequences are just as severe for Hagar as they are for Sing or Ruth, she begins to move the conceptualization of home out of the womb. She does not produce a child (in fact, the novel infantilizes her). And unlike Great Gram in *Corregidora,* who looks to the womb to produce hope for the next generation, Pilate rests the future of the Dead family upon Milkman's shoulders.

Hagar begins a ritual rampage, ostensibly to kill Milkman, after their breakup. News of this threat to her son's life once again sends

Ruth to Southside, seeking to defend him, where she confronts Hagar. Hagar is hurt and disappointed by Ruth's hostility. She tries to explain her motivation for stalking Milkman: "He is my home in this world"; Ruth retorts, "And I am his" (138). They are both wrong. Hagar cannot curl up inside Milkman any more than he can crawl back inside of Ruth. Ruth's womb was inhospitable even when his presence there was appropriate. Yet, in employing this imagery, Morrison signifies on Eva Peace in *Sula*—in this case, the mother would have the son come "home" to her womb, but he refuses to accept her on those terms. It is Pilate who states the wrenching truth neither woman wants to acknowledge: Milkman "wouldn't give a pile of swan shit for either one of you" (138).

This exchange encapsulates the inconsistencies that make it impossible for Ruth and Hagar to be at home and rooted. The scale they use to measure home is too restrictive because it begins and ends with the body—Hagar uses Milkman's and Ruth uses her own. Beyond the obvious futility of an attempt to do what is biologically impossible, both women fail to recognize that the nature of the womb is to thrust outward rather than to draw in. Despite the resonance of Baker's argument, the womb is not a vortex, "charged with extraordinary attractive force" (154–55), and any home conceived in these terms will not long endure. Home must be configured as a broader model that can accommodate progress and growth. The shortcomings of these women are not individual and personal; rather, they indict the African American literary tradition for its insistence upon the preeminence of patrimony over a woman's life and for its failure to appreciate the needs of the whole community in search of home.

Milkman's apathy toward Hagar is typical of his attitude toward women and reflects a social pattern that offers males privilege without responsibility. He no longer feels a connection to Hagar, so he responds to the threat she poses to his life by imposing his will upon her. His will invades her embattled psyche, displacing her desires with his. Milkman finally decides upon an ultimatum, "Either I am to live in this world on my terms or I will die out of it. If I am to live in it, then I want her dead" (129). It is a simple binary: she goes or

I go. This dichotomy, however, demonstrates his failure to integrate the blues sensibilities embodied by his aunt, which disrupt simple dualities. Neither is Hagar equipped with a language adequate to express her overwhelming emotions. Instead, paralyzed by her desire, Hagar is unable even to release her arms holding the knife above her head.

Hagar proves incompetent at killing Milkman. Rather than attempting to understand her motivations or to show compassion, Milkman is relentless: "'If you keep your hands just that way,' he said, 'and then bring them down straight, straight and fast, you can drive that knife right smack in your cunt. Why don't you do that? Then all your problems will be over'" (130). The knife becomes a surrogate for Milkman's penis, invading and violating Hagar's vagina. He wills her death by directing her to mutilate the passage that leads to her womb. Milkman is so completely self-absorbed that he is blind to his responsibility for Hagar's behavior and unaware of the power he wields over her life. His behavior mirrors Macon's toward Ruth, although Hagar's womb, which might hold the promise of the future, is apparently barren. Even her vagina has been emptied of pleasure. The journey to and from the uterus is a dangerous passage, threatened by male agents who show little regard for women or the fruit of the womb. Sing's womb is the cavern of dead flesh from which Pilate must escape and Ruth's womb is the site where Milkman's life is threatened by his father. Milkman's last encounter with Hagar signifies the continuing threat to the womb. But by not actually involving the uterus, choosing instead to operate on the plane of wit and will, this encounter also provides the segue that leads out of the body.

Finally, Morrison reinforces the image of the dead womb first represented in Pilate's birth and repeated and revised in the figures of Ruth and Hagar by moving into metaphor. The Butler mansion is a womb site that speaks of death and the Dead family past. "If metaphor," as Susan Willis maintains, "and much of Morrison's writing in general, represents a return to origins, it is not rooted in a nostalgia for the past. Rather, it represents a process for coming to grips with historical transition" (264). The collapsing ruins of the

Butler house suggest a gangrenous womb, but the house also serves to shift spatial orientation away from the female body toward the materiality of the built environment. Retracing Pilate's steps in his search for a secret cache of gold, Milkman soon finds his way to the Butler's mansion, out of reach by car. Milkman must go the distance from the road on foot. He makes his way down a dark tunnel into an interior site deep in the woods. "He looked back down the path and saw the green maw out of which he had come, a greenish-black tunnel, the end of which was nowhere in sight" (240–41). It is a primordial place that is literally and figuratively larger than his mother's womb. He steps into the past, a time before his birth, into a place large enough to hold clues to his father's past and his grandfather's past too.

His unwitting quest for home begins with an allusion to the German folktale, *Hansel and Gretel*. While the familiar childhood characters salivate over a witch's gingerbread house, Milkman vomits from the stench of a different witch's house before Circe comforts him (as the two fictional forebears were similarly comforted) with the smell of ginger root. Now the only human occupant, Circe literally steps out of the past in a moment of what Susan Willis calls "funk." Willis defines "funk" as "nothing more than the intrusion of the past in the present" (280), but such moments play a vital function in helping Milkman to overcome major failings of his past. This "funk" also reads as the uncanny, which indicate for Siegbert Prawer "that we are nearing that dark, transpersonal realm of . . . [Jung's] collective unconscious, that realm of mythological forms where things and persons become magical, taboo, dangerous and yet full of the promise of enrichment and salvation" (14). Circe is far too old to be alive, yet she remains to watch the Butlers' house decay and to feed the dogs so that they can help assure the demise of this property. She wills herself to live in order to see this process through.

While Mary Rambo is an archetypal maternal figure serving to expand the male sense of home by staying in her place, Circe transcends that archetype. At the end of the novel the narrator of *Invisible Man* intends to run home, where presumably Mary remains available to receive him. Like Mary's, Circe's obligation is also in the home, but she transcends the limitations of her assigned black (female) place simply by staying there too long. The invisible man cannot return to Mary (in the body) although he retreats into her surrogate womb. Macon II, on the other hand, can literally return to Circe through the eyes, feet, and mouth of his son. This crucial distinction helps Milkman make the transition from egocentrism to social responsibility. Carl Jung asserts that our efforts should be to "connect the life of the past that still exists in us with the life of the present, which threatens to slip away from it" (157). The consequence of missing this sort of connection is "a kind of rootless consciousness" (157)—the kind that characterizes Milkman's life. As a signifier of the maternal, Circe *recalls* the past and provides Milkman with tangible evidence of his place within it. She is the cord that reaches through time and keeps the past from slipping away. That is why this midwife who never lost a baby (and only one mother) smells like "ginger root—pleasant, clean, seductive" (241).

More than magic, the smell of ginger suggests deep, strong roots, like those found in Southside. The luxury of air conditioners deprives the upwardly mobile middle-class African Americans of the smell that rides into open windows of Southside on the air: "there the ginger smell was sharp, sharp enough to distort dreams and make the sleeper believe the things he hungered for were right at hand" (185). The scent of ginger suggests the hope that the women of *Corregidora* believe is offered only in the womb. This root, like the herbs Ruth uses to bewitch Macon, works like black magic, enticing Milkman into the dark hull of the Butler house.

Milkman has an erection when he enters and climbs the stairs to meet Circe's embrace (242). He is aroused and succumbs to her seduction. In this seminal moment, Milkman enters and becomes present in his ancestral past. It is similar to the scene at the end of *Corregidora* when the distinctions between identity and time collapse for Ursa—"I didn't know how much was me and Mutt and how much was Great Gram and Corregidora" (184). Ursa's epiphany is the recognition that the ability to gain control over our past "had to be sexual." It has to be because rootedness is sexual; it is the present act we perform with our bodies to invoke the past and reach into the future through the process of reproduction. The womb, in this final configuration as the rotting shell of the Butler mansion, emerges as a place of thinly veiled yearning—the desire to be remembered, the longing to be productive, the need to live on one's own terms—placed in constant jeopardy by the corruption of material culture. Time threatens to destroy both the material environment produced as a monument to this yearning and the human life the womb promises to bear. The womb, first metonymic of the African American woman, becomes synecdochic for home and ultimately reads as a sign of decay brought on by the supreme investment in material culture. By demystifying the womb, the novel frees Milkman to go elsewhere in his journey home.

Kitchens: Open Outward

In *Song of Solomon*, the black hole is not the nostalgic, restful haven into which men fall to recuperate; instead, it is more directly identified with the black woman's body as a womb. Likewise, kitchen places are complicated by the presence of men who conspire, laugh, and talk through late evening hours. While there are numerous scenes that occur in the kitchen, I will discuss two brief passages: Circe's confrontation with Milkman about her commitment to the Butler household and Pilate's description of a man falling off a cliff in his kitchen. Together, these two scenes help us understand how Morrison continues to redefine the terms given to represent home by making the kitchen into a site of resistance. While Morrison demystifies the womb by reading it more literally, she mystifies the place of the kitchen by asking to suspend our disbelief. Analysis of these scenes will not provide a complete picture of home; however, it is a concise reading of the dynamics at work within the place of the kitchen and how those dynamics differ from kitchen scenes represented in the previous novels.

The kitchen is, of course, that place of domestic servitude within the white household assigned to the African American in the racist past. It is also an interior site crucial to developing kinship within the place of home. The kitchen fosters connections that help alienated people like Bigger Thomas or the narrator of *Invisible Man* to feel at home. For a moment, even Bigger lets down his guard when he sops his plate with his bread in the Daltons' kitchen. But Mary Rambo's and Mrs. MacTeer's blues kitchens offer only meager resistance to a huge white supremacist apparatus that distorts notions of home to its own ends. This apparatus continues to demand that an individual stay in her place (even when removed from an occupation as a domestic servant), which sexism and the legacy of slavery insist, for African American women at least, remains the kitchen. The blues kitchen that gives a measure of comfort to the invisible man proves unable to penetrate the madness that ensues in *The Bluest Eye*, a short time after Pecola's father rapes her on the kitchen floor. Cat Lawson, in *Corregidora*, is more aware than any of the other characters of how the kitchen works to victimize her. Unfortunately, awareness alone is not enough to compete with that despotism. Awareness must be accompanied by an effective means of resistance that might function, like the blues, to comfort individuals who are able to identify with this mode of expression; or that, like Circe (and her deep ginger roots), works to dismantle the authority given to the material environment of the kitchen altogether.

The image of the kitchen plays a significant role in America's historical development and expansion. It is not hyperbolic to assert that Circe's presence within the Butler household has global implications. While I am certainly not suggesting that a line leads from Circe to World War II, Amy Kaplan argues, after examining the writings of Harriet Beecher Stowe and others, that domestic rhetoric is a vital counterpoint to nationalist rhetoric. During the mid-nineteenth century, in particular, the language of domesticity suffused debates about national expansion. Kaplan says, "Women's work at home . . . performs two interdependent forms of national labor; it forges the bonds of internal unity while impelling the nation outward to encompass the globe" (587). Domestic discourse both redresses and reenacts the contradictions of the empire through its own double movement—to expand female influence beyond the home and the nation, while simultaneously contracting the woman's sphere to police domestic boundaries against threats from within and without. The movement inward, which in African American literature is a movement into the body, like the trend represented in nineteenth-century discourse, is really a subset of a larger, masculinist expansion. This outward thrust is fueled, in part, by African American domestic labor. Circe, then, arises out of this discourse as the localized black female figure who serves as the mechanism of American expansion. She must somehow become larger than her assigned station, root herself deeper than the nationalist movement, or simply outlive it in order to challenge the meaning of her place within the kitchen.

Although Circe does not actually appear there, the kitchen is a station that dictates how she is permitted to act within a given environment. Circe's assigned place in the Butler household is the black (female) kitchen, traditionally designated for African American women. Just as William Faulkner laments in his grotesqueries the emaciated landscapes in the fallen South and wrestles with the implications of race and servitude, Morrison depicts a sophisticated dynamic at work in the now defunct Butler household. Like Clytie in *Absalom, Absalom!*, Circe's presence within the household complicates our reading of the power relationships set in place to perpetuate and to disrupt racial hierarchies. As Homi Bhabha describes, "In a feverish stillness, the intimate recesses of the domestic space become sites for history's most intricate invasions. In that displacement, the border between home and world become confused; and, uncannily, the private and the public become part of each other, forcing upon us a vision that is as divided as it is disorienting" (445). The subjugated, eternal black presence within the household invites the question: Whose side is she on?

Circe disrupts the myth of the "loyal servant" who holds no personal ambitions by, among other things, harboring the children of the man the Butlers killed. She is a defiant figure who clearly understands her social responsibilities. Yet she endures like Dilsey in *The Sound and the Fury* to see "de first en de last" (375). Milkman misinterprets this dedication as her love of the Butler family and their home. When he confronts her with this perspective, Circe responds curtly, "They loved it. Stole for it, lied for it, killed for it. But I'm the one left. Me and the dogs. And I will never clean it again. . . . Everything in this world they lived for will crumble and rot" (249). Circe's dedication is not to the Butler family, but to overseeing the demise of their estate. When faced with financial ruin, the remaining Butler killed herself. Circe has witnessed the end of the family line, but she wants to see the material legacy destroyed, too. She and Milkman sit together in the last room in the house that has not yet been demolished. Her dedication is a triumph of the human spirit over the unconscionable pursuit of wealth.

Circe's survival symbolizes the African American collective will to endure nearly insurmountable conditions. The rotting hull of the Butler mansion, then, represents the inevitable demise of an unjust system that dehumanizes its agents and contorts a testament of their strength into a sign of their weaknesses. Yet, in this mixed-up world of kitchens and home, Circe's fate remains tied to that site. The kitchen is a cauldron built upon the myth of white supremacy, maintained by male dominance, and threatened by the potential for treachery. If the kitchen no longer can be trusted to serve the home, then the integrity of the home is compromised. By expanding Circe's presence from background in the national landscape to foreground within the domestic portrait and by pushing the limits of mortality, Morrison creates a figure that is simultaneously real and mythical. When Milkman leaves Circe, the authority of the black (female) kitchen place is all but dismantled.

Pilate is another character who refuses to behave according to the demands of the kitchen. Having discovered that she is virtually alone in the world, she throws "away every assumption she ha[s] learned and beg[ins] at zero" (149). At an age when most people have already stopped imagining, Pilate discards her beliefs. She does not allow preconceived notions about people or places to dictate her experiences. This unburdening is the crucial step in "opening up" the kitchen for Pilate. Philosopher Martin Heidegger suggests that "spaces open up by the fact that they are let into the dwelling of man" (157). The kitchen maintains its authority over the lives of its subjects by obscuring obvious conflicts and functioning within a set of given expectations. Because Pilate has rejected those expectations, she is able to accept the improbable story her employer offers:

> He said he couldn't figure it out, but he felt like he was about to fall off a cliff. Standing right there on that yellow and white and red linoleum, as level as a flatiron. He was holding on to the door first, then the chair, trying his best not to fall down. I opened my mouth to tell him wasn't no cliff in that kitchen. Then I remembered how it was being in those woods. I felt it all over again. So I told the man did he want me to hold on to him so he couldn't fall. He looked at me with the most grateful look in the world. (41)

Pilate does not concern herself with the impossibility of falling off a cliff inside the kitchen of his home. Instead she opens up her mind to receive his version of events and enters into the scene just enough to attempt a rescue. Pilate is receptive to his belief that he is falling but resistant enough to remain standing safe in his kitchen.

This kitchen, like any other social space, is fraught with inconsistencies. Heidegger offers the following example to explain the quality that space has of becoming quite malleable given the right set of circumstances: "If all of us now think, from where we are right here, of . . . [a particular outdoor place], this thinking toward that location is not a mere experience inside the persons present here; rather, it belongs to the nature of our thinking *of* that . . . [specific site] that *in itself* thinking gets through, persists through, the distance to that location" (156). Personal experience with a particular site formulates an understanding that coalesces in the *making* of that space. The space becomes "real" in the present environment even when the physical site is at some distance.

As liberal as Heidegger's reading of dwelling places is, Morrison manages to imagine something larger through the medium of fiction. In the kitchen scene Pilate describes, Morrison challenges Heidegger's notion that building produces locations that "allow spaces" by moving further into the immaterial. Pilate asks, "What difference do it make if the thing you scared of is real or not?"

(40–41). Regardless of what the built environment of walls and floors *allows*, belief is more powerful. The man's belief in the cliff and Pilate's investment in that belief defy the laws of physics operating inside the kitchen. The wife of the man Pilate is working for is not as receptive to her husband's perspective. She makes Pilate release him before he feels safe on his own. Once Pilate lets go, it takes him "three whole minutes to go from a standing upright position to when he mashed his face on the floor" (41). Space, according to Henri Lefebvre, signifies "dos and don'ts;" but the logic of place that dictates that a man cannot fall off a cliff while standing in his kitchen is disproved by the incontrovertible evidence of the amount of time it takes him to fall.

The place of the kitchen is opened up for the man because it contains a dangerous cliff from which he is falling. It is also opened up for Pilate because she accepts this alternative viewpoint as viable. Once walls (or in this case, floors) are undermined as effective barriers that restrict what logically can happen in a place, they lose their authority. Lefebvre asserts that "rather than signs, what one encounters here [in a social space like a kitchen] are directions—multifarious and overlapping instructions" (142). Lefebvre's "dos and don'ts" signify an infinite range of possibility; the viability of what is *not* real, in Pilate's experience in this kitchen, undermines the legitimacy of what seems to be more tangible. The monolithic walls that seek to confine those assigned to a particular station, such as the kitchen, become permeable and wholly unreliable. The price of his wife's disbelief in the possibilities is her husband's death. What the location allows is challenged by the reality of that event. And truth moves beyond what has been built as a kitchen into what is experienced as belief.

City: The Ghetto

Finally, the city returns to the notion that home is accompanied by a dark copy of itself. This copy usually remains a mere shadow, but at moments, the ghetto Jes Grew out of control. Then we see the blackening of the great white city in Wright's *Native Son*—white made more palpable by its thick covering of blizzard snow. Funk erupts and uncannily forces us to confront the reality that the distance between the bourgeois aspiration of owning the "Erie Lackawanna" and giving up nearly everything there is to own is as thin as the flip side of a dime. The blues is one means ghetto inhabitants like Pilate use to reverse the field of play—submerging the city and recalling the ghetto.

In *Song of Solomon*, the city is neither an adversary, as it appears to be in *Native Son*, nor an obstacle course, as it is in Ellison's *Invisible Man*. Nor does the city simply serve as the backdrop against which Morrison in *The Bluest Eye* and Jones in *Corregidora* can foreground the increasingly interior space of home. The first part of *Song of Solomon* is set in a modest-sized city in Michigan. The city is small enough for people to know who lives there but Northern enough to accommodate a burgeoning black middle class. It is here that the siblings Macon and Pilate Dead first appear. I have already discussed Pilate's mythical birth and how she liberates herself from the tyranny of the kitchen. What remains is to situate Pilate within the framework of home.

In the introduction of *Blues Ideology*, Baker records an epiphany he experienced during his study of African American culture, "I found myself confronted with a figure to ground reversal. A fitting image for the effect of my reorientation is the gestalt illustration of the Greek hydria (a water vase with curved handles) that transforms itself into two faces in profile" (2). This metaphor describes for Baker the relationship vernacular productions have to dominant culture. While I have already offered an involved critique of Baker's blues matrix in the previous chapters, I consider this image appropriately applied to the characters Macon and Pilate. If the novel, according to Morrison, is about "a journey from stupidity to epiphany, of a man, a complete man" (quoted in Grewal 62), then it bears upon Baker's theoretical black whole.

A man becomes "whole," in Baker's terms, or "complete," in Morrison's, when he is immersed within a culture that knows its *whole* self. The play between the figure and the ground captured in the image of the Greek hydria is represented by Morrison in the interchange between Macon and Pilate. As Denise Heinze observes, "Pilate, as manufacturer of a pleasurable product and an adversary to squeezing money out of neighbors—though not necessarily of making it—is the aesthetic antithesis of her utilitarian brother who makes people pay dearly for a basic necessity so that he may live in comfort" (85). Pilate's rejection of material concerns diametrically opposes Macon's total investment in "owning things." Yet neither character can be understood fully except in contrast to the other. Without becoming involved in the intricacies of rhetorical composition and design, I suggest that Macon is presented as the figure and Pilate as the ground (or vice versa); each is created through the play between positive and negative space. Together they represent the *complete* picture.

In other words, as a product of the ghetto—by which I mean a site encouraging the return of that repressed African identity—Pilate is *unheimlich,* while as an inhabitant of the city—by which I mean that normative metropolitan lifestyle involving work and play within a fairly densely populated built environment—her brother, Macon is *heimlich.* These German terms, *unheimlich* and its apparent opposite, have no ready equivalents in standard English. In a discussion about the uncanny in literature, Siegbert Prawer offers these definitions for the word *unheimlich*:

> (a) The 'un-homely', that which makes you feel uneasy in the world of your normal experiences, not quite safe to trust to, mysterious, weird, uncomfortably strange or unfamiliar. In this sense, *unheimlich* has frequently been used as the equivalent of a word that would seem to be its opposite, the word *heimlich* meaning 'secret' or 'hidden.' And from here, from this dialectical tension between *heimlich* and *unheimlich,* we arrive at a second meaning which has interested several writers from Schelling to Freud: (b) The 'un-secret', that which should have remained hidden but has somehow failed to do so. (6–7)

If Macon is the figure who has safely concealed that private, black part of his experience since his father's violent murder, Pilate is the figure who exposes the same Africanist past. The siblings split after their father is killed defending his land from the jealous and greedy Butlers. Macon resorts to the city in order to build a place of his own that cannot be stolen, and Pilate retreats into a ghetto experience that keeps "her just barely within the boundaries of the elaborately socialized world of black people" (150).

Macon's pursuit of things results in the acquisition of numerous properties that he manages from his desk in Sonny's Shop. However, Macon lives on Not Doctor Street, which town legislators and town maps only acknowledge as Mains Avenue. The street was renamed by Southside residents, patients of the only African American physician in town, in part because none of them lived there. The African American community is largely housed within Southside until the doctor's distinct social position situates him economically and geographically outside the predefined parameters of the general black populace. With his entrance the community has grown more complex than that which can be effectively contained within the Southside; so it must accommodate the doctor's social and physical proximity, integrating him into the communal landscape. The doctor's house expands the African American sense of place and Macon envisions himself, as a property owner, a suitable heir to his estate; "entertain[ing] thoughts of marrying the doctor's daughter was possible because each key [in his pocket] represented a house which he owned at the time" (22). Macon's success at integrating himself into the existing landscape suggests that he has found a place for himself in this growing city.

Macon's labor to establish a place of his own culminates in considerable wealth, but it also alienates him from the other black people in the community. A man's labor, according to Karl Marx, can take "on its own existence . . . it exists outside him, independently, and alien to him . . . it stands opposed to him as an autonomous power. The life which he has given to the object sets itself against him as an alien and hostile force" (quoted in Prawer 18). Macon works to "own things" so that those things will "own other things" and he can own himself and "other people too" (55). Unfortunately, material gain alone is not enough to satisfy the human longing for rootedness projected onto the place of home. The physical distance of his house on Not Doctor Street from the properties in Southside is mirrored by his emotional and psychological distance from Southside residents. Ironically, his labor turns against him, holding him outside of the community that reaps the fruit of his harvest.

Macon hordes dwelling structures in an attempt to fix his established place within the city and makes routine public displays in order to maintain it. His behavior proclaims to those around him that he *has* a home; conversely, his behavior accuses them of being without. But this is not the perspective from the Southside. According to Homi Bhabha, "To be unhomed is not to be homeless, nor can the unhomely be easily accommodated in that familiar division of the social life into private and the public spheres" (445). Bhabha is referring, of course, to the *unheimlich,* which I identify with the ghetto. Although Macon now lives in the house that expanded the horizons of the local African American sense of home, he feels challenged by Southside. Even the buildings themselves seem defensive at times: "Scattered here and there, his houses stretched up beyond him like squat ghosts with hooded eyes. He didn't like to look at them in this light. During the day they were reassuring to see; now they did not seem to belong to him at all—in fact he felt like the outsider, the propertyless, landless wanderer" (27). Under the shadow of night, the black, ghetto place comes to the foreground. Macon, in his refusal to identify with it, becomes more clearly the disinherited city dweller, wandering aimlessly about someone else's land.

Originally, ghettoes were ethnic enclaves carved out by Jews who settled in Italy, segregated communities where they could preserve their religious practices and culture. By the time of the Crusades, the increasingly militant medieval Christian church began to formalize the ghetto by imposing legal restrictions on Jews. However, as Louis Wirth observes, "The historians of the ghetto are usually inclined to overemphasize the confining effect of the barriers that were set up around the Jew, and the provincial and stagnant character of ghetto existence. They forget that there was nevertheless a teeming life within the ghetto which was probably more active than life outside" (19). In twentieth-century America, the ghetto has come to be associated with the disenfranchisement of African Americans. Yet, like the original Jewish settlements, the black ghetto is teeming with life. Like Bhabha's description of the "unhomely," the ghetto cannot be fixed within simple dichotomies. In fact, in this scene Macon is ghettoized by his status as outsider. The figure who is secured, both literally and figuratively, by the keys in his pocket slips into the background. In the evening shadows, Macon becomes dispossessed of his land.

Macon's attempts to own property so that he can own himself and other people prove finally as impotent as Bigger's carnivalesque inversion of the Daltons' home. Bigger is thwarted most immediately by his ignorance of the furnace mechanics but more significantly by the larger institutional structures that predetermine his failure. The billboard's policing eye, which insists that "you can't win," may be absent from Macon's setting, but his wholehearted internalization of Eurocentric systems of power leaves him nearly as vulnerable as Bigger. While Macon's response to his father's murder may not be physical violence, it is far from self-affirming.

More remarkable in this context is his sister Pilate's practice of respecting the people and things she encounters as she meets them within their own environment. Heidegger might define this quality as "sparing" and "preserving": "Sparing . . . takes place when we leave something beforehand in its own nature, when we return it specifically to its being. . . . *The fundamental character of dwelling is this sparing and preserving*" (Heidegger 149). Pilate spares by meeting an individual where he is (as she does, for instance, with the man in his kitchen) and preserves by respecting the contributions others bring to encounters. Thus Pilate, according to the terms laid out by Heidegger, *dwells* in the land.

This sense of dwelling is manifested in Pilate's incessant wandering after her father's murder and her subsequent estrangement from Macon. Her lack of attachment to any particular place is contrasted with her ability to locate and retain significant communal signposts. Pilate keeps the inheritance of her home literally in the form of her father's bones and figuratively in the partial narrative of the blues text. She is an agent of the blues like the classic blues artists Angela Davis considers in *Blues Legacies and Black Feminism*. Davis explains, "The women who sang the blues did not typically affirm female resignation and powerlessness, nor did they accept the relegation of women to private and interior spaces" (20). Pilate's journey continues to affirm the new pattern of expansion rather than retreat, supported by the expressive mode of the blues. "And Pilate embodies the image of the black blues woman, for her song of the lost man, flown away, departed, leaving the beloved behind in suffering and pain" (Skerrett 195).

That she continually interprets her world through the lens of the blues song (as she does on the day of Milkman's birth at the opening of the novel) keeps her perspective from being forgotten. Gurleen Grewal, borrowing her vocabulary from Baker, suggests, "Pilate's blues song and its referent, the historic/mythic flying African, depicts the despairing Robert Smith with blue wings; it succeeds in unifying, in 'an Afro-American expressive field' (Houston Baker's phrase), people as far removed from each other as the genteel Ruth Foster Dead and the poor Mrs. Bains, Guitar's mother" (70). The blues does indeed have the potential to unify disparate individuals into a community.

By using material wealth as a signifier of his superiority over those who do not have access to the same capital resources, Macon cuts himself off from the support of this community, leaving himself vulnerable in its presence. In his effort to hasten his trip from Southside, where he feels like an outsider, Macon passes in front of Pilate's house, where her song meets him in the street: "He was rapidly approaching a part of the road where the music could not follow, when he saw, like a scene on the back of a postcard, a picture of where he was headed—his own home. . . . There was no music there, and tonight he wanted just a bit of music—from the person who had been his first caring for" (28–29). The sound of the voices lures Macon, under the cloak of darkness, to Pilate's window, where he can secretly watch his extended family. Susan Willis suggests that Pilate's house gains its value within the novel because of its contrast to Macon's. "The utopian aspect of Pilate's household is not contained within it, but generated out of its abrupt juxtaposition to the bourgeois mode of her brother's household" (Willis 273). The music forces Macon to confront the image of his own home. Macon considers his own sense of isolation in contrast to Southside generally but to these women specifically. Yet, "as soon as man *gives thought* to his homelessness," Heidegger maintains, "it is a misery no longer" (161). Macon recognizes his own homelessness and allows Pilate's blues song to bridge the chasm between the siblings, at least for as long as the singing lasts. Scenes such as this one illustrate how borders become confused.

As children, Macon and Pilate face the world together, knowing that they are at odds with everyone else after their father's murder (including Circe, who had harbored them for a short while); they make a coherent unit for the time being. Before long, however, the murderous disruption that initially set them together against the world destabilizes even that last remaining certainty. Their father's farm having been stolen, their parents both dead, and their safety tenuous, when Macon and Pilate disagree on whether or not to take the mortally wounded hunter's gold, the final thread of unity that bound them is nearly completely severed. Yet years later, as Macon is pushed into the background by the ghetto of Southside at dark, he seeks solace in the shadows beneath his sister's window. While he may be standing outside the home, it is his identification with the people inside as family that resituates Macon in relationship to Southside. By allying himself with this household of women, he is able to use proximity and his ties to Pilate to identify with the ghetto and to assuage his feeling of loneliness.

As he stands outside Pilate's window in the darkness, Macon's sense of alienation melts away. For this instant, he becomes part of the ghetto. Meaning is created in the interchange between the siblings. This scene depicts a black whole—a fleeting moment of recognition that Macon and Pilate come from the same source. Unfortunately, this moment is tragically brief and leaves the distinct revelation that the city alone does not satisfy the yearning to be a "complete man," and neither does Pilate's ghetto lifestyle. But we see the potential for the same blues that draws Macon to the shadows outside Pilate's window to bring him home.

So much of African American literature has been represented as a quest for home. I could have chosen any number of texts. For the sake of cogency, I have focused on a few works, drawn from a period in American history during the latter part of the largest mass migration the nation has ever known. African Americans were seeking a place of their own, and this postmigration literature depicts the struggle to deal with the knowledge gained in its aftermath. Hortense Spillers maintains that "Domesticity appears to gain its power by way of a common origin of cultural fictions that are grounded in the specificity of proper names, more exactly, a patronymic, which, in turn, situates those persons it 'covers' in a particular place" (266). Her reading of the domestic can be readily applied to *Song of Solomon*, with its central quest for the name of the father that has been lost over time through the carelessness of racism and the drive toward upward mobility. But in reaching for those material comforts that seem to be available to all who labor for them, we must be aware of what might be lost.

The nearly forty-year span of African American literature represented here culminating in *Song of Solomon* reveals that home is somehow beyond place, beyond life, and even beyond death. It is an un-selfconsciously black place where men and women live alongside the ghosts of their past. We cannot walk away without carrying the bones inherited from our years of struggle. Even so, we must be able to encode those experiences honestly, in order to pass the *complete* story to the next generation. Home is a *whole* place captured sometimes in song, sometimes in fleeting moments of recognition.

The blues, these authors seem to suggest, is the expression that best represents the African American's peculiar position within the mid-twentieth-century American landscape. The city that looms so large in the literature produced during the Great Migration is not home. The kitchen is far too stultifying and the womb is little more than a romantic notion. Yet these sites form the basis of an African American vocabulary about home. We are left with the ghetto—the poor, black enclave nevertheless teeming with life—and the blues. Morrison seems to be saying finally that we must be willing to accept the possibility that we may be damned to walk beside home in a nether region of shadows and ghosts—lurking near but apart from the place we call home. This realm belongs to the ghetto.

Works Cited

Baker, Houston A., Jr. *Blues, Ideology, and Afro-American Literature: A Vernacular Theory*. Chicago: University of Chicago Press, 1984.

Bhabha, Homi K. "The World and the Home." In *Dangerous Liaisons: Gender, Nation, and Post-Colonial Perspectives* (Minneapolis: University of Minnesota Press, 1997), 445–55.

Davis, Angela. *Blues Legacies and Black Feminism: Gertrude "Ma" Rainey, Bessie Smith, and Billie Holiday*. New York: Pantheon, 1998.

Faulkner, William. *The Sound and the Fury*. New York: Vintage, 1929.

Grewal, Gurleen. *Circles of Sorrow, Lines of Struggle: The Novels of Toni Morrison*. Baton Rouge: Louisiana State University Press, 1998.

Heidegger, Martin. *Poetry, Language, Thought*. New York: Harper and Row, 1971.

Heinze, Denise. *The Dilemma of "Double Consciousness": Toni Morrison's Novels*. Athens: The University of Georgia Press, 1993.

Jones, Gayl. *Corregidora*. Boston: Beacon, 1975.

Jung, Carl Gustav. *The Archetypes and the Collective Unconscious*. 2nd ed. Princeton: Princeton University Press, 1969.

Kaplan, Amy. "Manifest Domesticity: No More Separate Spheres!" *American Literature* 70.3 (Sept. 1998): 581–606.

Lefebvre, Henri. *The Production of Space*. Trans. Donald Nicholson-Smith. Cambridge: Blackwell, 1991.

Morrison, Toni. *Song of Solomon*. New York: Signet, 1977.

Prawer, Siegbert S. *The 'Uncanny' in Literature: An Apology for its Investigation*. London: Westfield College, 1965.

Spillers, Hortense J. "Mama's Baby, Papa's Maybe: An American Grammar Book." In Winston Napier, ed., *African American Literary Theory: A Reader*. New York: New York University Press, 1990, 257–79.

Index

Willis, Susan. "Eruptions of Funk: Historicizing Toni Morrison." In Henry Louis Gates Jr., ed., *Black Literature and Literary Theory*. New York: Routledge, 1984, 263–84.

Wirth, Louis. "The Ghetto." In Joe T. Darden, ed., *The Ghetto: Readings with Interpretations*. Port Washington, NY: National University Publications, 1981, 15–26.